D0070024

On the loose

On the

loose

BIG-CITY DAYS AND
NIGHTS OF THREE
SINGLE WOMEN

Melissa Roth

WILLIAM MORROW AND COMPANY, INC. / NEW YORK

It is the policy of William Morrow and Company, Inc., and its imprints and affiliates,
recognizing the importance of preserving what has been written, to print the books we
publish on acid-free paper, and we exert our best efforts to that end.

Library of Congress Cataloging-in-Publication Data

Roth, Melissa.
On the loose : big-city days and nights of three single women /
Melissa Roth. — 1st ed.
p.   cm.
ISBN 0-688-15801-3 (alk. paper)
1. Single women—United States—Case studies.   2. Single women—
United States—Attitudes.   3. Urban women—United States—
Interviews.   I. Title.
HQ800.4.U6R68   1999
305.48'652—dc21   98-49942
CIP

Printed in the United States of America

First Edition

1   2   3   4   5   6   7   8   9   10

BOOK DESIGN BY JO ANNE METSCH

www.williammorrow.com

Introduction

"**What's wrong with** all those men in New York?" Casey Barr's uncle wanted to know at her younger cousin's wedding. "Why isn't my beautiful niece walking down that aisle?"

Lots of people are wondering why Casey and the roughly fifteen million other lovely nieces in their twenties and thirties are not walking down the aisle. But no one ever thinks to ask the question, Could this be by choice?

Despite the magazine headlines, bookstore displays, talk show topics, and sitcom jokes, it may be that this generation of women is — consciously or unconsciously — staving off marriage. According to the U.S. Census Bureau, women are waiting longer than ever to marry, and larger numbers of adults will never tie the knot. In 1997 a survey by *Glamour* magazine found that during the past two decades the percentage of female Americans aged twenty-five to thirty-four who have never married has more than tripled in the last two decades. And according to a survey by the presidential pollsters Penn and Schoen for *New York* magazine in April 1998, more men than women are looking for serious relationships in the big city.

What about the current generation of "marriage-age" women? Are they commitophobic? Are they too busy playing the field? Are they waiting in vain for the perfect man? Or are they simply too happy being on their own? One thing is certain: more of them are staying single.

I set out to spend a year in the life of three single women in their late twenties and early thirties — the height of the "marriage anxiety" years. I wanted to find three "eligibles," women who met the same criteria used to define desirable husbands. I found three women who are smart, attractive, glamorously employed, funny, and interesting. They have a healthy outlook on their single state, yet they are still struggling to reconcile all the contradictions about their lives: the images and the messages, the envy and the pity, the freedom and the yearning for something more.

I wanted to find out why these women, like so many others in their twenties and thirties, are still single. I wanted to see if they felt free simply to enjoy living the moments of their single lives. And I wanted to see if they experienced the panic and the loneliness that are so often assigned to them.

I myself am a member of the "marrying age" generation, born in the late nineteen-sixties. The time has come to buy *The Rules* and snare a bachelor. My clock is ticking, they tell me. But I am also a product of *Free to Be . . . You and Me*, one of the millions of kids weaned on the songs and stories that were the seventies' answer to Aesop's fables. For several of our early years, my brother and I mimicked the famous voices on our eight-track. "I want to be a *fire*man," I would announce in my Marlo Thomas voice. "What am I, a loaf a bread?" my brother would giggle, until chocolate milk came out his nose.

One of the stories was about a princess whose father insisted she marry a prince. She wasn't sure she wanted to get married; she wanted to see the world first. So she cut a deal with her king dad: she would race all the men he had in mind for her, and if she won, she would be free to do as she pleased.

"Faster and faster Atalanta ran . . ." a breathless man narrated. "Huff-huff-huff." Atalanta pulled ahead of the pack. Then Young John from the Town came from behind to tie her. She fell in love with him. She was free to. But Atalanta left to see the world, and Young John went off on a voyage. "Perhaps they married, perhaps they didn't," the narrator concluded. "Either way, she lived happily ever after." At thirteen, I joined the track team.

My girlfriends and I took coed gym and played organized sports: soccer, softball, track. We took coed classes, lived in coed dorms. We dated recreationally, because we felt we were allowed to. After college, we moved to cities with friends or by ourselves, for the jobs and the excitement, to "see the world." We had our own earning potential, our own credit cards, our own leases, our own lives.

But sometimes it's difficult to reconcile the joy of all this with the books and TV shows and articles that give the single life another spin. Hollywood and the media often tell us that singlehood is only a transitory phase—one that, for women, should be passed through as quickly as possible. We are still told that we need a ring, a most-eligible man. All the rest is just window dressing; it is simply about playing hard to get.

Yet many women, left to see life through their own lenses, actually enjoy their single lives. It's not that they don't have anxieties and letdowns, and it's not that they don't ever want to get married; it's just that there is something to be said for the freedom and the adventure and the *possibilities* that come from living a life all your own. And there is something to be said for the happily-ever-after that is right now.

Casey Barr, Anna Kendricks, and Jen Carroll are three women who grew up with the *Free to Be* messages; and for various reasons, they are still seeing the world—living in big cities, working at careers, exploring all the options.

THESE WOMEN WERE not easy to find. To be sure, there are millions of "eligible women" out there, but I set out to round up three who lived in different cities, worked in different fields, were different ages, and had different personalities. They also had to be forthcoming with the details of their personal lives, and they had to trust me—a stranger with a license to spill.

To scout them, I went "woman shopping." I patrolled friends' wedding showers, eavesdropped on conversations at thirtieth-birthday parties, scoped out summer share houses. At one point a friend took me to the glass-encased balcony of her Wall Street firm and we stared out over the trading floor. "How about that one?" I asked, pointing to a chuckling brunette surrounded by three Charlie Sheen types. "Married," she said, shaking her head. "What a waste," we both agreed.

Eventually, I found three women who met all the criteria. They did not know one another, but they had a few notable traits in common: they all came from intact families (pure coincidence); they all attended public schools in suburbia; and now they all have big jobs that involve travel, good salaries, and interesting work.

Their having "big jobs" actually created one enduring problem: talking to a pesty interviewer about their personal lives was not something they always had the time or inclination to do. To boot, there was nothing in it for them. They all wanted their identities to be disguised, so there was to be no glory (not even revenge). We couldn't pay them—this was not *The Jerry Springer Show*. There would be no groovy MTV loft apartment, not even a Monica Lewinsky–type photo spread in *Vanity Fair*. They had to agree to offer up the most intimate details of their personal lives for one year—all for the higher purpose of truth in singledom.

A tough bargain. But they embraced the project enthusiastically. My three subjects and I hit the town together—sampling parties, bars, boardwalks, and work events. We sat down for long dinners, talked about childhood, the news, jobs, TV shows, and men. I would call or E-mail them every other week and spend time with them whenever I could. They would introduce me as their "friend," in town from New York. I would listen carefully and try not to say too much. Then I would disappear into the bathroom with my pocket pad and furiously scribble notes.

There were *some* benefits for them along the way. At times, they seemed to be living their lives with a little more fervor. And they seemed to gather some personal insights along the way. "This is like free therapy," Jen remarked after a conversation about her childhood. "Am I going to *find* myself soon?" Anna asked my answering machine one day. "I can't remember the name of the guy I went to see *Boogie Nights* with," Casey announced at the end. "Could you look that up in your records?"

But there were plenty of times when they simply did not want me around, did not care to focus on "being single," or did not feel like sharing another intimate detail with me and untold others. "I don't have on-the-record sex," one of them snapped after a particularly nosy question. (I tried to persuade her: "Don't you read the papers? We *all* have on-the-record sex now.")

Most of all, they all had bigger priorities: stressful jobs they are devoted to, and sisters and brothers and friends and pets to answer to. And each of them, at different points, decided that she wanted to save some of her stories for her own purposes — a screenplay, a grandchild, a real therapist who doesn't say "That is so *great*" after a wretched date detail.

I understood their reservations, but I also had a book to write. So I was patient, and I would call them when I knew they couldn't screen. The truth is, I was enmeshed in their lives. I would stop in the middle of my day to wonder if Jen was going to fall for the hustling young filmmaker. "That reminds me of one of my women," I would tell friends over dinner. "She has a thing for coach men." I would write things like "shaggy D.A." and "tantric sex?" on yellow stickies that would turn up hours later on the subway seat next to mine. And, of course, I lived in constant fear that they would run off and get married.

Through hours and hours of conversations, I got to know these women as friends. I began to approach their stories less as a journalist than as a peer, sometimes getting into their heads, sometimes getting stuck in my own. Liberties were taken: it was agreed from the beginning that I would change names and certain details to respect the privacy of the women and the people in their lives. As a result, some of their friends have become composites, and some of our own conversations became scenes. But throughout, I've tried to stay true to each woman's stories, her distinctive style of speaking, and her thoughts as she presented them to me.

Casey, Anna, and Jen were not told much about the book or why they were chosen; I did not want to steer their conversations or confessions in any particular direction. Sometimes they seemed to tell me what they thought they should be telling me, because soon they would contradict themselves. They could be at once brazen and timid, invincible and vulnerable, victim and perpetrator.

And, perhaps not surprisingly, their comments and actions echoed the daily contradictions on the magazine racks we all passed each day: HOW TO KEEP A MAN and GET SINGLE were side-by-side headlines one month.

So here they are, the "big city" adventures of Casey, Anna, and Jen. After spending a year with them, I believe you'll have a better understanding of why so many women are still *On the Loose.*

March

Eligible: suitable or desirable for marriage.

—*Webster's Third*

MARCH 22, 1997, is the vernal equinox, the day when the sun crosses the equator and the season of fertility begins. In medieval times, the new year began on this day, marking the point when winter ends and the earth is reborn.

In Los Angeles, the arrival of spring is about one thing: apparel angst. The end of March is awards ceremony time, and awards ceremonies are about dresses. For Jen Carroll, the most exciting of these events is the independent film awards, held each year on the Saturday before the Oscars under a big tent on the beach.

Jen is a twenty-nine-year-old development executive at a Hollywood studio. She is always on the lookout for viable scripts — scripts that will make lots of money. She sits in a sunny office, wears an operator's headset, and pushes buttons to take calls, talk plots, drop figures. Then she pushes more buttons and meets people for lunch. At least once a week, she is obliged to go to some Hollywood event most of us only get to watch on *E.T.* "Most of the guys I meet," she says, "wear shiny black shoes and more hair gel than me."

Jen grew up in an L. L. Bean town outside Boston, full of boys in bowl cuts and camp shoes. She herself has a half-girl, half-woman face, big blinking brown eyes, and strong Irish cheekbones. She moved to L.A. from New York just over a year ago, and lately she has found herself drifting toward the young "indie" crowd, moody low-budget actors and tortured writers. "They're the thinking woman's crowd," she explains. "They don't look down your dress when they talk to you. Not many men out here can manage that."

Several of her current interests should be at the awards, bespectacled boyish men who went to impressive schools. "You know the type," she says. "You can't tell if they're being funny or making fun of you."

Appearances still count, however, and "the Indies" provokes the greatest dress crisis. The basic black number just won't cut it. Nor will anything too trendy, too "Oscar wannabe," Jen explains. And you can't spend much money, either. These are professional flea market shoppers.

Duress. The morning of the event, Jen's sister Becca arrives at her house at nine A.M., carrying a Starbucks nonfat grande latte, double shot of espresso. There is work to be done. She heads straight for the bedroom to see what Jen has laid out for round one: a long, black straight skirt with a shiny Chinese brocade top. Jen sips the foam off her coffee and twists her hair as she awaits the verdict.

"Where's the *flesh* here?" comes the response from the bedroom.

Becca works for a film production company, but she is thirty-three and married, and she skips these events. She still loves dressing up her younger sister, a favorite childhood hobby. When they were in elementary school, they played "bridesmaids," and Becca would drape them both in tablecloths and curtains to wobble down their hallway in their mother's heels. Five years ago, Jen traded in the tablecloth for a Laura Ashley dress and stood by as her sister married a grown man with a bowl cut.

Now when Becca dresses her, she needles her into "working it." "She is always trying to get me to hike up my skirt or unbutton my blouse . . . show midriff," Jen says. "I usually go along with it, but I can't be embarrassed. And I'm not going to have my belly hanging out."

When they were in high school, Becca threatened to tell on Jen when she caught her wearing a miniskirt to a football game. "I was not about to let my little sister become a *sleaze*," she laughs. Today she is rummaging through Jen's closet trying to find something, well, mini-er.

After a few rounds, they reach a settlement: a nude-colored strappy dress with a thigh-high slit and a clingy black sweater. The dress is Becca's idea. The sweater, Jen's. Jen pulls her brown hair back into a low ponytail, a few strands escaping to her face. Then she pokes two chopsticks into her hair clip, a final stab at "indie."

At noon, Jen's date pulls up in an old Chevy convertible. It's Emily, her friend from work, and Jen moans when she sees her get out of the car. "Will you look at her outfit! She just makes me look so . . . Connecticut. Where is that Japanese kimono thing?"

Emily is wearing a filmy blue embroidered sundress, tiny blue-tinted sunglasses, and platform slip-ons. She is always the envy of everybody on the awards ceremony–circuit. She mixes the perfect palette, paints the perfect portrait, and somehow strikes the perfect balance between appropriate and cool. Jen throws on a pair of square-framed sunglasses with a buggy-yellow tint. After a half-hour of party predictions and two more shots of espresso, they are on their way.

They drive down Santa Monica Boulevard in Emily's old convertible, listening to indie music, punching the rewind button over and over, repeating the only song they actually like. "Shady lane . . ." they sing (they know only the refrain), ". . . everybody wants one." Their voices quaver a little as they pull off the boulevard and spot the big beach tents.

Wobbling down the red-roped runway, they try not to look at any of the ninety photographers whose cameras dangle listlessly from their necks. "We're nobodies," Jen says of the awkward "entrance" she has grown accustomed to making. "They can spot a nobody car when it pulls up." Still, she catches herself staring down at the red carpet, a coy celebrity affect, except that she is just trying to make sure she doesn't trip on a cable cord and end up in some bloopers show, slit ripped up to her ribs.

At the end of the entrance ramp, Jen and Emily part. They head to separate bars. "The bar wait is one of the highlights," Jen explains. "You're mushed in with the crowds, forced to talk to whoever might be waiting for a drink next to you. It's major eye-contact time." She has a moment with one of her men, a short, mop-topped chain-smoker in the corner. He holds her gaze for a few extra seconds, then turns away and exhales a big loop of smoke. She flinches and turns back to the bar.

She orders a cranberry and seltzer, a fake drink. "I don't like to get drunk at these things anymore. It's my only insurance against embarrassment." Then she spots Bridey, an old friend from New York. They give each other air kisses, then admire each other's dresses. "You look *fabulous*," they say in mock L.A., and then spend several serious minutes studying each other's contraptions. Bridey is wearing a sheer strappy dress with strappy shoes—open toes and open breasts. (It's all about lumps.)

Jen asks about friends back East. "How's Dennis? Is he still into Buddhism?"

"Mm, no. He's into AA now. I think the ratio is better there."

"Oh, no. Well, I hear you've moved on. Lynn tells me you're in love?"

"Well . . . yes. It's official." Bridey holds out her hand.

"Wow! Congratulations—it's beautiful," Jen says, taking Bridey's fingers. "I mean, it's huge! You must be so excited."

"Yeah, I'm just a little freaked out these days," Bridey says. "You heard about Lori and Rob?"

"*No.* Not them. They were great together."

"I know. They got married at twenty-four, before any of the pressure set in, and I always thought they were the real thing. I thought I was going to be planning her baby shower any day. Divorced at thirty-one. She had no idea." Bridey shakes her head and sips her drink.

"I can't believe they're getting divorced. And to think, Courtney is getting married."

"Courtney? The one who hooked up with every guy in the summer share?"

"I know. Twisted. The people we thought had the most perfect marriage are getting divorced at thirty-one. The biggest party girl we know is getting married after six months."

"What is it with all these six-month quickies?"

Jen shakes her head. She is still trying to imagine being divorced.

"I think it's about dog years," Bridey answers her own question, staring into her drink. "People turn thirty and they convert time to dog years. The quickies happen because the men suddenly decide they're ready. All their friends get married, and they have nothing to do anymore. No one to go out with. They want to lock in a buddy who won't leave them for another woman."

"It's really about the male clock, isn't it?" Jen says, eyeing her carefully.

Emily comes over toting a tall, blond, ponytailed man, presenting him to Jen like a retriever with a pheasant. "When Emily brings someone over to me," she explains later, "it's usually because she's scoped him out and decided he was too young for her." Emily is thirty-seven. She's moved on to men. Jen is impressed with her find. He's a little oversized, but he has the grin of a sixteen-year-old. There's just one problem: he's wearing the sneakers, the blue Chuck Taylors with the star and the chevron. "I draw the line at fifth-grade sneakers," Jen says in her gym teacher voice. "But I guess guys out here wear them as a sort of creative badge. Like, 'I don't have a job-job where I have to wear real shoes.' "

Bridey recognizes the man from her old job. "Well, hello there, Sir James," she says, smacking him playfully in the gut. "I saw you pull up in that two-seater. They're calling it the 'me-people' car. You can't pick anyone up in the airport in that little number."

"Exactly," he says.

"Me-me-me," Emily jeers. "I'd offer you a lift, but there's just no room for you and the DVD player."

Sir James turns to Jen and squints. "How do I know you?"

This is L.A. for *What have you been in?* Jen knows. She asks him if maybe they met at one of Bridey's parties in New York. No, no, that's not it. Then he asks her if she's been on *Chicago Hope*. "He thought I was the actress who pushes the cart around!" she cries later. "It's so *annoying*. You don't exist here unless you're a B actress on a TV show."

Jen tells him that she works for a studio, and as she describes her job, his eyes widen and his head tilts earnestly. "The problem with these events is that you can't tell if people are scamming for work or scamming for sex," she explains later. "And rarely can you think they are scamming for anything else. The friendliness is always a little suspect."

Halfway into the awards ceremony, Jen and Emily take their seats at their assigned table. James soon joins them, carrying drinks and a chair. He talks in Jen's ear throughout the ceremony, narrating the event. "When Muhammad Ali got up to get his award, he started singing that song from third grade—'floats like a butterfly, stings like a bee.' I was probably the only one at our table who thought it was cute. Everyone else was giving him the hairy eyeball."

By the end of the ceremony, Jen starts to get a little embarrassed. Still, she agrees to look for James later that evening at the party for *The English Patient.* When she gets home to change there is a message from Nate, the man she likes to call her future ex-husband. He wants to know if she'll meet him at a record release. Horn-rimmed and smart, Nate moved to L.A. for a TV production job six months ago, leaving behind a girlfriend of five years in New York. They were in the midst of a long-term breakup, but he's having a little trouble with the breakup part, and so he goes back every four weeks to visit her. In between, he calls Jen under the guise of being lonely-transplant friends. "Then we get together, have a little too much to drink, and start kissing. We never talk about it. I don't want to be the miffed woman. But I'm miffed. I'm starting to really like him. He'll call me up the next day and start talking about his girlfriend again as if nothing happened . . . or maybe because something happened."

Jen decides to meet Nate "just for a little while." She gets into her car and drives down the Sunset Strip to the Viper Room club. Her mood drops a little when she hears that her favorite nineteen-year-old valet just left to be in a movie. The club is dark and full of dates. When she finally finds Nate, she whispers hello but refuses to look at him. "I'm mad at myself for agreeing to meet him." After about a half-hour of silence, Nate asks her why she's being so "distant." "I shake my head, mumble 'no reason' into my drink, then get madder. 'I've just been thinking a little too much lately,' I say. Long pause. I can tell he's sorry he asked. Too late. So I tell him he needs to make up his mind about where his head is at.

" 'I know, it's really unfair, isn't it?' he says.

"I tell him I don't want him to have to dump his girlfriend just so we can hang out (lie), but I don't play second fiddle very well, and it really makes me feel bad. He just stares into his drink. 'So until you figure it out,' I say, 'let's just be friends.' He nods his head and then tries to apologize. Next thing you know, we're watching *Saturday Night Live* on his couch, making out. Typical. Meanwhile, I completely forgot about Sir James."

Anna

THE SPRING EQUINOX also marks the point of perfect balance, when night and day are of equal length. This doesn't mean much in San Francisco. The bay looks like a giant bog, gray and smoky, and it's hard to tell exactly if it's day or night or something in between.

Anna Kendricks and her friend Lizzie are walking toward the Marina Green, down by the Golden Gate Bridge. Anna moved here two years ago when a West Coast advertising agency recruited her to be a management supervisor. Now she oversees national consumer products campaigns and a staff of three, working nine-hour days and traveling every two weeks for client meetings. Most of the time she works out of the agency—an old lofty warehouse building with high brick walls and skylights. There are people walking by her office who look a little like Gary from *thirtysomething*. They wear jeans and throw Nerf balls into small plastic hoops in the upstairs rec room.

Anna herself looks as if she stepped out of an old Levi's ad—dusty 501's and a familiar blue-eyed face framed in dusty-blond hair. She is part California sunny, part New York edgy, but she is actually from the Great Plains. She grew up in a wide-open frontier town with schoolteachers and insurance brokers and grain farmers. "There was a lot of trust," she says. "We never locked our house."

At thirty-one she has been married and separated, part of the wave of twenty-something couples whose marriages falter just as the third-wheel single friends disappear into domestic bliss. She married her college boyfriend, but after a secure transition into official adulthood, they realized they were not much more than friends. They finally separated two years ago, just before Anna moved out west.

As a newly single woman, Anna has had to make new friends — male and female. Lizzie used to work for Anna as an account executive. She is twenty-six and funny, and they swapped stories and impressions in Anna's office, laughing until they were hunched over. Pretty soon, it became clear that they were not getting much work done, so Lizzie was moved down the hall to the food account group.

Now they do all of their laughing on the weekends. Lizzie likes to visit Anna's neighborhood. Lizzie lives in the Castro, a gay neighborhood, and lately she has found herself staking out construction sites. "Yellow hats. I can spot them five blocks away," she confesses, shading her eyes. "I walk by them on my lunch break. I just need to be reminded that I am, in fact, a sexual object."

Anna lives in Russian Hill, an old Victorian neighborhood that was once a burial ground for the city's seal hunters. After growing up on the Plains, Anna has developed an attachment to hills. She likes knowing she is above sea level. But Lizzie likes to drag her down to the flat townhoused stretch by the marina. The Marina District is full of windblown sailing-skin types and overgrown fraternity types. Their common denominator: rock-ribbed heterosexuality.

On the way to the water, they stop at a small wooden news shack and flip through the papers. A twelve-year-old boy was expelled from the San Francisco Science Fair for neglecting his fruit flies. Twelve army officers have been charged with sexual harassment. A female fighter pilot was charged with having an affair with a married civilian. A Houston businessman has launched a catalog of wealthy forty-year-old Texas bachelors. . . .

Anna announces that she is heading to Texas again for a client meeting. She got pulled into a new business pitch for an Austin high-tech account a few months ago, and the client really liked her. Now the client wants her involved in the campaign.

"Does the bad cowboy have any bad friends?" Lizzie asks, lifting her sunglasses as they walk toward the bay.

The bad cowboy is Ethan, the thirty-seven-year-old Texan illustrator Anna hired to draw the storyboards for the high-tech client last November. They met when she went to Austin for the pitch, and since then they have been having a five-month phone flirtation. Ethan has a strong, carved face, and he hunts and fishes. He also builds things.

Ever since Anna visited Austin last November, she has come to believe that Texas is where all the straight men have congregated. San Francisco has a few straight boys, but Texas has cavalries of straight men. "Austin coffee shops," she tells Lizzie. "That's where his friends go. They sit by themselves and swig straight black coffee. None of this latte crap." Lizzie and Anna have decided they've had it with San Francisco's café culture. They're on a mission to meet straight-black-coffee men. Bad cowboys. They are willing to fly for this.

They walk up Polk Street and head to their favorite breakfast spot, an old soda fountain diner that feels like a Norman Rockwell painting. They grab the last two swivel stools at the counter and order egg-white omelets and caffeine-free diet Cokes.

Just as the food comes, two guys walk in wearing baseball hats and college T-shirts. "Don't look," Lizzie whispers to Anna, dropping her chin to her chest. "The Jeweler." The guys slide into a booth and search the diner for their waiter, and one of them spots Anna at the counter, looking. "Hey there," he says cheerfully from across the diner. Lizzie is forced to look up from her omelet. "Oh, hey!" she says waving and chewing.

Lizzie dated the guy in the Notre Dame hat for about a month last year, and the first time they fooled around he asked if he could give her a "pearl necklace," the kind made out of . . . *excitement*, helped along by . . . cleavage. From then on he became known as The Jeweler. Anna and Lizzie are in the business of naming things: The Suds Buster, The Thirst Quencher. No one gets by them without a tagline.

The Jeweler comes over to the counter, gives each of them a

kiss, and begins to massage Lizzie's shoulders as he tells them about his new software job. When Lizzie tenses her back in discomfort, he starts in on Anna. She drops her head and rolls it around. "Could you do my neck?"

Lizzie starts to giggle. She had forgotten about The Jeweler. He was *very* friendly. And very into the neck region. She looks over at his friend in the booth; he is smiling back at her, a sort of demented, young-Jack-Nicholson grin. He looks like he could be The Bedazzler.

They finish their omelets, wave good-bye to the boys, and walk over to Chestnut Street to meet Jeanne, another work friend. They're headed to Tiburon, the tiny peninsula town that juts out into the bay on the other side of the bridge. Whenever it is warm, they like to sit on the crammed deck of Sam's Anchor Café drinking Bloody Marys and waiting for the fog to lift so they can admire their blue-and-white hill city across the bay.

"You wouldn't know it from looking at it, but that pile of buildings over there is the most righteous place on earth," Lizzie says chewing on her celery stick after they arrive. The San Francisco skyline is just starting to poke through the fog.

Lizzie is very philosophical. She likes to contemplate how people can drink something called Bloody Marys and why people make semen necklaces and whether San Francisco can turn liberals into conservatives.

"Uh-oh," Anna says, "I met an investment banker once who used the word 'righteous.' Don't tell me it's happening to you."

"I'm serious," Lizzie says. "This place has a way of throwing off all your reference points. Everyone comes here thinking they're liberal and open-minded, but then there's always someone around the corner waiting to pounce, waiting to accuse you of being Satan."

"Competitive righteousness," Jeanne adds. "This place is actually more righteous than the Bible Belt."

"Brad asked me how I can work in advertising. He said he could never *exploit* people for a living," Lizzie says.

"Tell Brad you could never insult people for *free*," Jeanne says, now chewing on her straw. She has lived in the Haight for the last six years, and the counterculture is wearing on her. "And tell Brad you could never exploit other people's money." Brad is one of San Francisco's trust fund bohemians. He wears tattered Brooks Brothers shirts and Tevas and throws Frisbees in Golden Gate Park during the week.

"Lizzie, you shove stuffing down people's throats for a living, sodium puffs," Anna interjects. Lizzie has been working on a boxed-instant-stuffing campaign. "You *are* Satan."

Anna likes her philosophy with punch lines. The last time the word "righteous" came up, it turned into a fight about religion. She is in the process of finalizing a divorce; she doesn't want any more fights. She decides to change the subject.

"I'm sick of feeling guilty about not mountain biking and windsurfing every weekend. I just want to sleep in and read my magazines and drink Bloody Marys. There's something unnatural about this need to be outside all the time."

"They don't mountain bike or windsurf on *Suddenly Susan*," Lizzie says pensively.

"That show is so unrealistic," Anna says. "Susan would never fall for Judd Nelson. He made a lot of bad movies in the eighties."

"And there are no men in this city who look like that photographer," Jeanne adds.

"Uh-uh. All the sexy men go to sexy cities like New York or Denver or . . ."

"Austin," Anna adds.

"Yeah, Austin."

If San Francisco can turn liberals into conservatives, it can also make otherwise healthy women boy crazy. Anna and her friends claim they were never as focused on sex and dating before they moved to San Francisco. This is because everywhere else they have lived, there were plenty of straight men looking at them and thinking about it for them.

Not here. The tables are clearly turned. With the ratio in the straight man's favor, all of the straight women do the thinking for them. The men just live, get ogled, shrug their shoulders, and get laid.

So Anna flies to Texas. "It's all about ratios."

Casey

MARCH 22 IS also the first day of the zodiac year, Casey Barr explains. The first constellation lines up in the Milky Way, and the astrological year is ready to start over.

Casey is a green-eyed Pisces with an irrepressible smile and a smooth, gliding voice. She never really paid much attention to horoscopes until her gynecologist pointed out that the female cycles are the same as the lunar laps. Four weeks for ovulation—the moon's full lap around the earth. She decided there had to be something to all of that orbiting.

Some sort of planetary force pulled her to New York twelve years ago. She was booking music acts at Ohio State when she met a band manager with a Dutch accent who said to look him up if she ever came to New York. A year later he found her an entry-level job in the music business. Now thirty-three, Casey handles media relations for a record company. It's her job to see that the new releases on her company's label get lots of press. To do this, she spends most of her days on the phone and many of her nights at music shows.

Casey just got back from a video conference in San Francisco. She hasn't eaten anything since yesterday, when she lost her appetite. Just a week ago, she was counting the days until Stefan would be back from Tokyo. Stefan is the Dutch man who helped her land her first job. He's become her mentor over the years, taking her out for sushi lunches and talking about music reviewers and foreign cities and *Billboard* charts.

First she fell in love with the sushi: red and orange squishy fish wraps. Stefan introduced her to sashimi, ginger, and cold sakè drinks in cedar boxes. Then one day, Stefan and the sashimi got rolled up together in her mind, and she fell in love with him.

"Stefan hasn't exactly cared for his vessel," she says, wrinkling up her nose over drinks one night at a "kava" bar in the Village. She's trying to explain how this all happened. "He dresses like Austin Powers. He's losing his hair. But the man can work a waiter. He's smart and charming, commanding. And I guess on some level he makes me feel protected. I know that, professionally at least, he'll never let me drown."

Two months ago, after a late dinner and three porcelain carafes of sakè, they ended up back at his apartment. He waited until after they had sex to tell her he was still married. He'd been meaning to get a divorce for four years, he said, and he finally had a reason. Casey hid from him for a week. He sent flowers to her office, then left a message explaining that the divorce was in the works. Then she hid for *two* weeks. Finally one day last month he showed up at her apartment covered in snow, holding a handful of long-stemmed somethings, and she let him in.

"I've never been courted like this before," she explained one night while he was away. "He sends notes and flowers all the time. It's kind of hard for me not to reciprocate."

By the time he left for his business trip, they had been spending every other night together — at movies and music shows and sakè bars. But that was before he left for Tokyo. And that was before she left for San Francisco.

What happened was this: a cameraman in the hotel pool the day after the conference. She lowered herself into the shallow end, and when she looked up she saw a young Ryan O'Neal, like a male mermaid, half submerged and staring back at her. He had watery-blue eyes and strong, tanned arms, draped across the back of the pool. He smiled at her and didn't say anything. He dropped his head back, closed his eyes, and appeared to fall asleep. Then he stopped her as she was leaving the pool and asked if she wanted to take a drive to Muir Woods.

She spent the rest of the day in the passenger seat of his car, her knees pulled up to her chest, talking to a spot on the windshield. She couldn't look at him. He was too much to look at from too close. Then he told her about his Austrian mother and his soccer team and his Rolling Stones collection.

Casey spent her teenage years in Europe and Illinois, and sometimes this makes it hard for her to relate to people. She hit puberty surrounded by foreign accents and foreign boys, and she learned to make friends through music—first Kiss, then the Rolling Stones—and sports: track and coed soccer and dodgeball. "The flirtations began there—soccer or dodgeball. Ping-Pong. We would pummel one another with whatever ball we could find. That's how we communicated." It was during all this ball-thrashing that Casey developed an early taste for foreign boys. "They were just sweeter and more romantic. It was okay to be a Casanova. The American boys were always posturing—it was not cool to fall for girls; girls fell for them."

At Muir Woods, an old-growth forest just north of the city, Casey and the cameraman hiked through a grove of redwoods. When they reached an overlook with a view of the ocean, she stared at his knapsack and tried to imagine what was in each zipped pocket. He didn't turn to kiss her until later, when he dropped her off at the airport.

Back home in her apartment, she is sorting through her stack of mail. There is a letter from Stefan, written on hotel stationery: "If only you were here." She leaves the letter in the pile by her front door and collapses on the couch. She wants to talk to her brother Brett.

Casey is close to her family. Her father worked for an international retail company when she was younger, and the family moved around a lot—she spent fifth grade in Germany, eighth grade in Switzerland, and tenth grade outside Chicago. "It was hard moving . . . all the time. But we learned pretty quickly that good things would always come of it." Her younger brother Brett is her chief counselor, talking to her twice a week from St. Paul, Minnesota. He puts a midwestern balance on what can sometimes be a highly distorted New York life. Her younger sister calls every Sunday from

Virginia and puts her four-year-old on the phone. "Having my younger sister get married first definitely caused some anxiety," Casey explains. "But my family has always been genuinely excited about my life. They make me feel like my life is great the way it is. And they've never encouraged me to stay with anyone if I wasn't happy."

Brett upholds that standard when Casey tells him about her weekend.

"I didn't plan this," she sighs. "I think people come into your life for a reason. I'm supposed to learn something from this."

"Case, you put up with Bruce for almost four years. Learn from that," he tells her.

Bruce was one of the "anyones," her last serious boyfriend. They met when she was twenty-five. "It was very love-at-first-sight," she recalls. "We stared at each other from across this dark bar. He had this Flock of Seagulls haircut and a look in his eye. There was something really familiar about him." Six months later, Bruce moved in. "It was great. We fixed up my apartment together. I would go out and do my music thing during the week, and then on weekends we would stay in and order Chinese and pay-per-view."

Two years into the relationship, Bruce joined the marketing team for a single-malt liquor company, and he became deeply loyal to his product. He had boxes of it in their apartment, and they were always open. He found a neighborhood bar and became a regular on the nights when Casey was out for work. "That was fine, but you don't have to stay out until five in the morning and pass out on the living room rug," she says, her even voice teetering just a little. She finally got the courage to talk to him about it. And when that didn't work, she finally got the courage to kick him out.

"I KNOW," she tells her brother when she remembers the ending with Bruce. "I can't jump back into that. I think I want a whole collection of men."

"I would really love to see you pull that off," Brett laughs.

Casey picks up Stefan's note again. He said he was due back on Sunday, the very next day. She leaves her apartment and goes to back-to-back yoga classes. She needs to exhale a lot of stuffy air from the bottom of her lungs before she can figure out what's next. This big man—Stefan—has been a sheltering presence in her life for over a decade. He practically raised her. Her whole sense of things, people, the next life phase—it's all wrapped up in him. And now she is entranced with a faraway man she can hardly speak to.

Brett asks Casey if she could ever leave New York, move out west. "I don't know," she tells him. "I need to run around for a while. If I were to leave town, live somewhere else, I would feel the 'settle down' pressure. But I'm just not scared here. I have had great relationships, but I'm not done kissing all of my frogs yet. And each frog is an upgrade. I'm all for continual upgrades."

Brett tells her she should find someone and upgrade together. She says she is not ready for that.

April

In most literature, if the heroine is having
great sex she is doomed—Anna Karenina and
Madame Bovary are two of the most famous
examples. I don't know of a literary heroine
who experiences a great deal of pleasure
and lives happily ever after.

—Mary Gordon,

quoted by Liz Smith

ANNA IS SITTING alone in a coffee shop in Austin, tapping her
nails against a diet Coke waiting for Ethan, the bad cowboy. A
small-screen TV above the counter is broadcasting images of the
flood-sunk Dakotas, only a few hundred miles from where she grew
up. Her parents are safe and sound in sunny Florida, but she can't
seem to stop fidgeting.

The first time Anna heard Ethan's voice, something in her spinal
cord sank. "He has a deep baritone voice, and he started talking
about art exhibits. Here's this baritone cowboy, and he's an artist
and he's talking about exhibits I should go see, and I'm picturing
him as my wise and beautiful museum guide."

She started to tell everyone in the office about him, playing his
messages to the assistants and making up stories about how they
were going to ride palomino horses (naked, of course) across the
plains of Texas. So everyone decided that there had to be something wrong with him. "You are going to get all worked up about
some big voice, and then you'll meet him and he'll come up to
your navel," Jeanne said. His nickname around the office then
became The Dwarf.

By the time she first flew to Austin, Anna and Ethan had exchanged life stories. Sitting in her client's office, she spotted a striking man with dark blue eyes walking by the door. He stared in at
her for a moment, then disappeared, and she lost her train of
thought. Five minutes later, he stopped and stood in the doorway.
"He was wearing this hat, not like a ten-gallon hat, about three
gallons, and he looked like Henry Fonda in _The Grapes of Wrath_."
The man waved to Anna's client, then held out a big hand. "I'm
Ethan."

That afternoon, he invited Anna to come see his studio, which also happened to be his apartment. "I show up sweating in one of those little silk Banana Republic T-shirts," Anna recalls. "It's a little more form-fitting than . . . you know what I mean. He's wearing a white linen shirt and he's got big steaks thawing on the counter and some kind of fresh basil-y sauce on the stove. Meanwhile, the baseball game is on and there's this Paul Bunyan magazine on the table." At this point, The Dwarf was renamed: Renaissance Cowboy.

After a tour of his paintings and prints and photographs, Anna excused herself. She went into his bathroom, turned on the water, and searched the cabinets for makeup and tampons. Nothing. Then she spotted something black on the doorknob. It was a hair scrunchie. Ethan doesn't have a ponytail. She didn't stay long after that.

But since then, she and Ethan have talked every week. She told him about how she left her husband, how he's involved with someone now, how she screwed the whole thing up. He told her about his ex-girlfriend, how he pushed her away. Then he told her he felt a strange connection to her.

By the time Ethan shows up in the coffee shop with his two friends, Anna is plotting to run across the street to a liquor store and buy an airplane bottle of Jack Daniel's to pour into her Coke. Floods in the heartland, a day in client meetings, and now she has to face the man who has been rising like the Mississippi in her mind for the last five months.

Instead she slides back into the booth, and a bald man named Rob moves in across from her. Then a lanky redheaded man takes the spot next to her. Ethan grins from his spot diagonally across the table. After the introductions, the bald man starts telling her about himself. She doesn't remember asking, but now he is explaining that he is a venture capitalist and a pilot. She listens to his stories about engine problems and makeshift landings, wondering if this is supposed to be some kind of a setup. Why did Ethan insist on bringing his friends? He didn't have to let them corner her.

After half an hour, Ethan suggests that they go to a pool bar, but when they get there, the bald man slides in next to Anna again. Another half-hour of stories about air traffic and wind patterns, then she excuses herself and goes to the bathroom. When she returns, only Ethan is waiting for her.

"I think my friend likes you," he says grinning.

"Why is that so funny?" she asks, sliding in next to him.

"Well, 'cause I sort of had my sights set on you."

"Well, why didn't you do anything about it?"

They start kissing in the bar, about a minute before the lights come on. "Let's get *out* of here." Anna says, ducking the glare.

They end up back at Anna's hotel. She's walking across her room to turn on the dim lamp when he tackles her onto the floor. He lifts both of her arms up over her head, then starts pulling open the button fly on her jeans. She giggles nervously, then stops.

"By the end of my marriage, the only sex my husband and I ever had was friendship sex. We didn't want to hurt each other's feelings, so we'd go along with it. There was not a lot of intensity." But this was different. This was . . . unexpected. "This guy is very controlled on the outside. Underneath this placid exterior he's this stormy, out-of-control brew. It's very exciting to see someone that excited. I kept thinking I was going to get to his next layer. I was very into unearthing him."

And then he became deeply concerned about unearthing her. Renaissance Cowboy.

The next morning they order room service—yolked eggs and black coffee—and he tells her about his girlfriend. When she asks him what happened to the "ex" prefix, he explains that things have been very on and off between them. He's very confused about the whole thing. "But I want us to be able to be honest with each other," he says.

"I thought we *were* being honest with each other," she says flatly.

They spend the day at a sportsman show. Ethan likes to go on fly-fishing and hunting expeditions and tells Anna he wants to check out some new lures. A giant stuffed caribou stares at her as she walks into the coliseum, which is filled with booths and display cases. Large men are buying rifles and Budweisers. She is trying to picture her ex-husband there. Greg grew up in Manhattan. He's probably never even *seen* a fly fish before. Renaissance Cowboy is talking about shells and hooks and bull's-eyes. He stops to poke Anna's rib cage to show her where he would put the bullet. Then he squeezes her flank, the part he says he eats first. Cowboy fore-play.

By the time they get back to her hotel room, Ethan is placid and quiet.

"I have to tell you something," he says in his lowest voice yet. "I'm gettin' too close to you. I'm going to start pushing you away."

"Ethan. We were talking about moose meat. Should I be alarmed?"

"No, it's just that—I don't want to fuck this up. You're a great friend."

"Ethan."

"Yeah?"

"First of all, I don't usually have sex with my friends. Second, look who you're talking to. I'm still married, technically, and in love with my ex-husband . . . now that he's three thousand miles away and we've decided to divorce. I chose to live in San Francisco, the city of unavailable men. And I'm sitting across from you, king of the *Cosmo* commitophobe quiz. You don't owe me any expla-nations."

This is Anna's competitive dysfunction side. She has a few others. But at this point, she is starting to feel that she doesn't need this.

Back in San Francisco the following week, Ethan calls Anna every day. "I had an incredible time with you," he says her first day back. Then he explains that his mother was an alcoholic, emotion-ally unavailable to him, and now he's emotionally unavailable to everyone else.

"You see," Anna explains later, "all the women he's dated have ended up seeing shrinks and picking up these buzzwords and phrases. Then he latches on to them and uses them with the next woman he dates."

Ethan is retro-titled. He is back to being called The Dwarf. "The man is emotionally stunted."

Casey

"I'M DOING BREATHING exercises." Casey calls to report from a pay phone at the Cancun airport. She is trying to distract herself. "I'm so fucking nervous. What are we going to talk about?" In an hour the cameraman's flight is arriving. She suddenly wishes it were Stefan's flight, or Bruce's, someone whose knapsack doesn't make her flushed.

Casey and the cameraman exchanged E-mail addresses after their drive to Muir Woods. She discovered that it was much easier to talk to him in word-processed thoughts. They've spent the last three weeks typing careful notes back and forth about bands and videos and minidisks. Then he asked her if she wanted to meet him in Mexico.

Casey avoided Stefan for a couple of days after he got back from his last trip. They were both busy with work. Then he made a reservation for them at Nobu, the nicest sushi restaurant in New York. He sent a car service to pick her up at home and take her there, but even after the sakè and the ginger and the raw fish, she still couldn't bring herself to sleep with him. She told him she had to get up early and went home. Now he's on his way to Sydney.

The cameraman arrives safely, and after a stiff embrace, they begin the painful first minutes of "how was your trip" talk. Their first night together will be in a hotel on the beach. They are planning to drive down the coast to the Yucatan peninsula and hike to the Mayan ruins the following day. Casey gets excited at the thought of crumbling pyramids. As a kid, she liked to climb things—jungle gyms, trees, rocks. When she was a teenager, the things got bigger — steep cobblestoned streets and ski slopes. In high school, she climbed her house — sneaking in and out of her bedroom window in the middle of the night.

She's always had an insatiable curiosity about the unknown. She carefully packed each pouch of her bag — Swiss army knife, lipstick, condoms. She looks over at him when they are unpacking and realizes he has only brought one small knapsack. *Three days* in the same clothes?

Their first night together is rocky. She's nervous and self-conscious; she has to look him right in the eye. Things are rushed, both of them fumbling. "It was really clunky," she reports later. "He was definitely a guy who hadn't had a girlfriend in a while. Very high school. I was really missing Stefan." Then he tells her that he hates having to use a condom, and she tells him that they can't do without one. They fall asleep on opposite sides of the big double bed.

They wake up early the next morning and drive to the peninsula. Casey is still staring at the windshield, this time talking about pyramids and the Mayans and her sixth-grade social studies project. He's mostly quiet. They have to hike through a thick forest to get to the pyramids, and Casey stops once at the top of a hill to stare out over a canopy of mist. "Have you heard about the new digital handhelds with auto-tape editing?" he asks her as she pulls out her camera.

"No," she says, trying not to look at him. He's pulling a mini-cassette recorder out of one of his zipped pockets.

"Memo," he says (no kidding), holding the recorder up to his mouth like a walkie-talkie. "Handhelds, auto editing."

At this point, she is staring over at him. "I don't want to forget," he tells her.

A silent hour later, they reach a crumbling rock metropolis, and as they get closer to the central pyramid, they hear echoes of giggles. Against the dark village they see outlines of small people, circles of kids who look like Girl Scout troops on an overnight. Casey begins to climb the big steps up the pyramid.

"Where are you going?" he asks her.

"We're going to the top."

Silence. He stands still, one leg propped on a rock.

"This is the whole reason we came," she reminds him.

All around them are packs of ten-year-old girls who have spent the day climbing giant boulders. Her fantasy date says he's too tired.

"Fine. You stay here. I'm going."

An hour later she meets him back at the bottom, her face cold and pale.

The cameraman is obligated to explore things every day as part of his job. On vacation, he's doesn't want the pressure. The rest of the trip is a wash.

When she gets back to Manhattan, Casey buys a gallon of paint, Sunburnt Red, and a super-roller. She's been meaning to paint her bedroom for six months, and now she wants to fall asleep in a new apartment. She gave up Bruce for Stefan, and Stefan for some acro-phobic equipment junkie—all in a season's work. The cameraman calls three days later, and after ten minutes of stretched-out small talk, he asks her for the name of a New York video producer.

Jen

JEN HAS JUST found a great script—a drama based on the life of a female fighter pilot. With the Kelly Flinn story hot in the press, the time seems ripe for a female *Top Gun,* she told her boss. He loved it, so she can finally eat her lunch again. He's been going through a nasty divorce, and things have been a little tense around the office. For the first time in her year and a half in L.A., she feels safe from reproach. It's time to take a long weekend, and the only place she really wants to go is New York.

They say it's not a good idea to visit your old home until you feel you have a new one to return to, and the last time Jen visited New York, this was not the case. Los Angeles still seemed like someplace where she was vacationing, a very long spring break. Everyone she came across in New York was like a long-lost soul-mate. She was still secretly planning to stay, get a big fat job, and bunker herself away with Max, a pathetic acoustic guitarist she couldn't quite seem to shake.

Her last year in New York was hell, Becca regularly reminds her. She had a boring job at a giant media conglomerate, a deeply cynical ex-boyfriend, and a lingering affair with the guitarist. Becca wooed her out to L.A. with irresistible job leads, but she has always been afraid that Jen will leave her and move back East. She doesn't even like the idea of Jen's visiting New York. What if she meets someone? What if the mangy guitarist gets up on stage in his tube socks and begs her to come back? What if Jen thinks that she really liked hell?

As a preemptive strike, Becca suggests they go to Santa Barbara for the weekend, but it's too late. Jen has already booked her flight to New York.

Once her plane lands, Jen hops into a cab and heads for her friend Fiona's studio apartment downtown. Jen went to college with Fiona, a black-haired, blue-eyed New Englander who works in documentary film. When Jen still lived in New York, she and Fiona would throw "after-hours" parties at Jen's place in the Flatiron district. They invited their friends and a few people they had met out that night. If they spotted one of their crushes, they would send each other over—tag team—to invite him to the party. After one particularly lively night, Jen's living room looked like a post-prom basement, couples tilting into angles on couches, each pair oblivious of the next. From then on, Jen's apartment came to be known as the Pleasure Palace.

Jen and Fiona are telling Palace stories. There was the "O" man, the guy who turned his mouth into a capital O while he was having fully-clothed sex with Fiona in Jen's storage loft. There was the temp from New Jersey who tried to bring his passed-out roommate into Jen's bed with them. There was the guy who started crying immediately after he fooled around with Lynn.

There will be no more Pleasure Palace nights. Fiona has fallen in love. It was starting to happen just before Jen left for L.A.—a graduate student Fiona had met through her brother. Jen and Fiona are sharing French fries at the BonBon, a tiny diner in the West Village. Jen is talking about the men she has met in L.A., but Fiona isn't really listening.

"Which one is Nate?" she asks.

"Nate's my future ex-husband," Jen says, dunking fries into ketchup puddles.

"Jen," Fiona's voice drops. "That's not something you plan for."

"I'm just kidding. It's just my way of being playful about it. Nate is this guy I'm kind of into. I'm keeping it light. Besides, I live in L.A. now."

"What's that supposed to mean?"

"Well, the average life span of a marriage in L.A. is about eighteen months. My friend Emily says you should only marry someone you can imagine being happily divorced from."

"That's terrible," Fiona says, frowning. "People who plan for divorce will divorce."

"Well, it's not so terrible if you've seen it happen to half the people you know. And it's not so terrible if you were the kid whose unhappily divorced parents tore your arms out of their sockets. It's just a way to protect everyone."

"How about if you just marry someone you really love, instead of some Hollywood goon?"

"Fiona. You really loved Eric. Would you want to drop your kids off with him and the hussy right now?" Eric is the man Fiona fell in love with in college.

"I never would have married him."

"Oh, come on. You would have run off with him on crush party night sophomore year if he'd asked."

"Well, see. That's just it. You're wiser and more evolved when you're in your thirties. You see through that."

At thirty-one, their friend Bridey met a man she knew she didn't have to see through, and Saturday night is her engagement party at the Bubble Lounge, a champagne bar in TriBeCa. Her parents have rented out the downstairs wine cellar: brick walls, overstuffed couches, antique yellow lights. Jen shows up in a suede jacket, which hides a vintage slip dress, which is lined with a rib-sticking Nancy Ganz bodyglove . . . which means there is no room for underwear.

"Please remind me that I am not picking anything up tonight," she says when she sees her friend Lynn. They are both carrying small, stuffed wrist-handle purses and are laughing at each other. Lynn has swooped her hair up into a side-parted beehive, strands pulled across her forehead. Behind her is a silver-haired man in a plaid suit, probably Bridey's father. Next to him is a tall, stretchy woman in breathable leather. Barely breathable leather.

Marisa Tomei is there, standing behind Jen, but Lynn doesn't want to point. Instead she widens her eyes at Jen, hoists her chin in the actress's direction, and stomps her leg three times into the floor—a reenactment of Marisa's scene from *My Cousin Vinny*.

"What are you doing?" Jen says, staring at Lynn's foot.

"Behind you. Don't look."

"Mr. Ed?"

"No." Lynn says through clenched teeth. "Biological clock . . . tick tick tick." Now she is jerking her head, eyes bulging.

"My biological clock rusted," Jen giggles, champagne percolating to her head. "I don't have that leg thing . . . tick, tick, tick."

"*No!*" Lynn says, rolling her eyes. "Behind you, the girl from *My Cousin Vinny*."

"Oh. Marisa. I see her in L.A. all the time."

Celebrities have become scene backdrop to Jen, part of the decor. She has adopted a star-maker's indifference to the "properties." What she does notice is Evan, her last official "ex," patting the naked back of a tall, brunette woman. With his other hand he is combing a chunk of his rooster-red hair off his forehead.

Evan carries on about his new girlfriend, Catherine, during his monthly phone calls to Jen. He met her while pretending to read the *Utne Reader* at a Barnes & Noble café, a month after Jen gave him the "this is not really healthy" talk. Evan had become a catatonic fifties man. He read the paper, grunted, fell asleep by ten. Now he cooks artichoke casseroles, hangs out with Catherine's dad, goes to parties with her.

"Why do all the guys I date become these great boyfriends immediately after me?" Jen asks Lynn. The champagne buzz is starting to take a turn. "I'm training them, disciplining them, *dumping* them, all so these women can just step in and reap the rewards. They have their little crisis. And then the next woman they meet they want to lay down and marry."

Lynn is shaking her head. She just broke up with a forty-four-year-old real estate broker.

"I fired him," Lynn says when Jen asks about the real estate guy.

"You downsized?"

"Had to."

"He wasn't producing on the job?"

"None of his jobs."

"Sometimes you just have to let people go. Are you sure it wasn't a problem with the man-age-ment?"

"No. He had a pretty clear job des-crip-tion. Pretty basic."

Over Lynn's shoulder, Jen watches as Evan's girlfriend giggles, squints, shrugs, and drapes herself over the stuffed couch next to Bridey. Evan catches Jen watching him and excuses himself.

"I want you to meet Catherine," he says kissing Jen on the cheek. "She's a little nervous about it. I told her that you're both Hal Hartley fans. We went up to Vermont last week, and she brought that book. . . ."

Jen is no longer listening. She has popped out like a clutch. She is staring blankly past Evan when she notices a pair of Ben Franklin glasses across the cellar. They are propped on the nose of a sad, puffy-faced Irish boy—the product of too much rainfall. He looks like Boston. She takes another sip of her champagne and clasps her stomach.

"Jen, Bridey wants you to meet her brother." Lynn has come to rescue Jen from Evan. She drags her upstairs to the bathroom. Engagement parties can be stressful, and the disengaged must tend to each other. "What happened to the guy Bridey introduced you to in L.A.?" Lynn asks through the stall door. Two women are applying lipstick in the bathroom's mirror. They pause for Jen's response.

"Which one?"

"I don't know—some tall, blond thing."

"Oh, him. Not really my type," Jen says.

"Don't tell me—he called?"

The lipstick women giggle.

"Yeah," Jen smiles at them. "Complete psychopath."

"There's a fine line between a guy who calls, you know, like his mother told him he should, and the guy who just unravels before your eyes," Lynn says.

"Yeah. Flashers. Emotional flashers. Just, exposing themselves to the world."

"So, how many times did he call?"

"Oh, it wasn't that. Although, now that you mention it, he didn't bother to wait for me to call him back. I'm not a little rabbit that's waiting to be speared. I can dial a phone."

"It's hard to like a guy who appears to have no self-control."

"Yeah. It's just hard to see in others what you don't like in yourself. I mean, somebody has to have some control."

The four women smile at one another as they compete for the bathroom mirror.

Jen has been trying to figure out a way to tell Lynn that she is going to leave the party early. Max's band is playing at a bar off of Bleecker Street, and they usually get kicked offstage by the main attraction around eleven. Lynn can't stand Max, ever since he pulled out his guitar at Jen's birthday party to impress a guy from a record company. "I'll buy you a drink," Jen tells Lynn on the way out of the bathroom. "I have to leave in a little while. Fiona is dragging me to the Village to meet some actor who's moving to L.A. next month."

Lynn squints and gives Jen a suspicious half smile.

MAX'S BAND PLAYS in bars listed in *Let's Go USA*. People stand just outside of them, on Bleecker Street, and hand out fliers as if it's the state fair. Inside, the clientele wears Tommy Hilfiger rugby shirts—a European teenager's idea of American fraternity chic. Jen and Fiona head straight to the sticky bar and wedge themselves between two colorfully striped boys. Jen is mouthing the words to Max's songs. Max and Jen were never actually a couple, not in the exclusive dinner-and-a-movie sense. But they *saw* each other for about a year before she left New York, and she fell for him. He was smart and spectacled and he sang beautiful songs and he *picked* her, out of the crowd. How could she forget that?

Looking down the bar she spots Kevin, the band's manager, and goes over to give him a kiss. She turns her face to the stage as Kevin tries to talk in her ear over the music.

"Max's fiancée is here," Kevin says carefully.

"Oh, I've been dying to meet her!" Jen says, beaming. Jen had heard Max was *dating* someone, but she had no idea they were engaged. "What's she like?"

"You'd like her. She's smart, she's funny, and she hates Max." He smiles and waits for her to laugh.

"No wonder you like her," Jen says, chewing on an ice cube.

"Did I mention she has cash?"

"Uh, you didn't need to. And a big beautiful air-conditioned apartment. When is Max signing the pre-nup?"

"That would probably be a good idea," Kevin laughs.

Jen has one arm stuck behind Kevin, the other flagging the bartender with a twenty. As she talks into his ear, he moves in closer, placing a hand on her lower back. Suddenly she jerks herself away and runs back to Fiona, flinching.

"Is everything okay?" Fiona asks.

Jen shakes her head.

"What happened?"

"He just gave me the weenie treatment."

"Pressed himself up against you?"

Jen nods.

"*Eew.* Well, you did look pretty damn happy to see him."

"Fiona," Jen grabs Fiona's drink and takes a big swallow. "Max is engaged."

A tan, cologned man with wet hair moves closer, and Jen turns toward him and forces a smile. He holds out an open hand and tilts his head in her direction. She turns to Fiona for the reassurance she does not need. Then she turns back and takes the man's hand, and before she can give Fiona's drink back, she is pressed flat up against a large chest, one leg on either side of a very aggressive thigh. She's seen people do this at Rudolpho's in L.A. She decides the guy must be Argentine, maybe Ecuadorian. He sashays her around the bar for a few minutes, rolls her out, rolls her back in, then starts shimmying her to the floor. Suddenly she remembers her bodyglove, the bottomless body slip, which is shimmying its way up her hips. She breaks away, pulls her dress and slip down, and runs back to Fiona with her empty drink. Up onstage, Max is singing to a row of tiny blondes. They are mouthing the words to his songs. Audience recruitment, he will tell the fiancée later.

Anna

EACH YEAR IN early spring, Anna and her two closest friends from college, Ness and Gwen, go on a ski trip. It began with their spring break in senior year, when they were all single. For a few years in their twenties, each brought her significant other. But ever since Anna separated from her husband, they've decided to make it a women-only event.

When they were twenty-four, they spent a week in a cheap hotel in Breckenridge, a family resort in Colorado. Waiting at the chairlift at the end of a long line of screaming snowsuits, they swore that someday, when they were still childless, they would spend the money and go to Aspen. That day has arrived.

Ness almost canceled this year at the last minute — her husband thought they should go somewhere together. The two of them met at Anna's engagement party seven years ago, and they got married just as Anna was thinking about splitting. After hearing this, Ness ran out and bought a save-your-marriage book. Anna's announcement really threw her. She'd been sure they would be the perfect foursome.

Anna is now the only single one. When it looked as though Ness might back out this year, she thought about inviting Ethan so they could all have dates. Then she thought better of it. Aspen is very exciting. She might meet someone. Besides, she's been trying to wean herself from bad cowboys.

The first day on the slopes, the women have a little trouble adjusting to fun. Ness has not been away from her husband since last year's trip, and she seems to be going through withdrawal. Gwen got into a fight with her husband the night before she left, and she is unusually quiet. Anna is still depressed about the midwestern floods. Staring down at all the snow, she keeps imagining it melting into a river through her hometown. But she drags Gwen and Ness to a bar at the end of the day and buys them each a shot of orange vodka in the hope of perking up the vacation.

The next day, after the skiers' special breakfast, they stop off at a touristy photo store. Anna puts her face in the Garth Brooks cutout and Gwen puts her face in the Elvis cutout and the man behind the counter says, "Say cheesy!" and they do. Then two twenty-five-year-old guys come in and stare down at the developed photos. "Who the hell is that supposed to be?" one of them says, pointing to Garth-Anna.

The guys turn out to be ski bums living in Aspen for the winter. They work as chairlift operators and skiers' special chefs, but they spend most of their time on the slopes. One of them looks like Anna's first college boyfriend—drowsy eyes and curly brown hair and a shit-eating grin. She asks him to recommend some trails. "And now my two married friends are going to be skiing with these two college ski bums," Anna announces to Gwen and Ness as they put on their skis, "all because Anna's single."

The five of them head to the lifts, and Anna and the man with the drowsy eyes ride the chairlift alone together. They swing their skis and talk about where they're from. Anna tries to steer him away from the what-do-you-do question. She doesn't want to have to explain what a management supervisor does, how she's been in advertising since he was in puberty. The question doesn't come up. He is busy asking her about her skis and bindings and goggles.

An hour later, Anna is lost down a wooded side trail and Gwen is following her, screaming for her to slow down. "That man is a stone-cold fox. If you lose him I will *kill* you."

The boys are waiting with Ness at the bottom of the hill. They invite the three of them to a party later that night and tell them to bring their bathing suits. It's a hot tub party. "That's so seventies," Anna says, wrinkling her nose. When the boys disappear, she falls to her knees in the snow and tugs on Ness's jacket. "You have *got* to come with me . . . *ple-e-ease*? I don't meet *that* in San Francisco." Ness and Gwen are laughing and shaking their heads. "This was your idea!" Anna yells at Gwen. "You can*not* let me go alone."

At two A.M., Anna and Gwen tiptoe back into their hotel room, trying not to wake up Ness. They both have cold damp hair and smeared lipstick, and they are a little drunk.

"Where have you two been?" Ness says, looking at the clock.

"Making porn movies with the ski bums," Anna says, giggling. Gwen doesn't laugh. She made Anna swear she wouldn't say anything to Ness about the night. Ness would not approve.

It was just a tiny transgression—first base, really—but Gwen is afraid to call her husband the next day, afraid he will hear something in her voice. Things have not been going well between them. She was offered a big job in San Francisco a few months ago, and Anna heard about an ad job for her husband, but he wasn't interested. He has a so-so marketing job at a company in Philly, but he doesn't like change. Gwen craves adventure. "You're turning thirty-four," he told her. "You should be craving kids."

Anna's a little detached when it comes to other people's relationship crises. Lately she feels as if she's all fazed out. Besides, a few marital problems no longer seem like the end of the world to her.

She spends the last two days of the ski trip with the man with the drowsy eyes. He lost interest in her bindings and skis and became extremely fascinated with the rest of her. He even took two days off from the restaurant and borrowed a friend's condo for a night.

"The guy was clearly in his sexual prime," she reports later. "He could have gone on forever. And he was so damn sexy that no other effort was really necessary on his part. It's clear that his whole life women have just been so fucking thankful he gave them a minute of his time that no one's bothered to notice that he's not even trying.

"But two days of sex, and I never wanted to see him again. He cured me of this 'best sex in the world' trip with the bad cowboy, and that was all I needed."

Casey

THE SUPER-ROLLER races up and down Casey's bedroom wall, splattering sunburnt paint on her face and hair. She wants to be done. After her Mayan misadventure, she made a vow that she would try to relax and shed layers: dead skin, heavy boyfriends, bad karma. Her acupuncturist, Hank, looked at her posture and told her that her chest center was very closed. "Hank," she told him, "my men are not cooperating." He shifted her shoulders back and poked tiny needles into her chest. "Why do you let them get to you?" he said, shaking his head. Then he told her to wear a rose quartz necklace. "I think he was trying to keep me from getting coldhearted," she says.

Stefan is back in New York for a solid two months, so he has lots of restless time on his hands. He is a music publisher now, which means he makes money on artists' songs by selling the rights around the world. He calls Casey at home, then at work. She can't bring herself to sleep with him. He thinks they're just taking things slowly.

On the other hand, she can't imagine meeting anyone new right now. She is exhausted, and she doesn't trust herself. Besides, meeting someone new requires a lot of imagination, and hers is dried up at the moment. The problem is that Casey has never been a big believer in celibacy. Sex is like exercise and showers, a necessary regimen for the body and soul.

Sometimes Stefan seems to sense this, because the following week, he sends her two dozen roses with a note: "Let's start over."

"The man is really into abundance," Casey explains, a little embarrassed. "He can't do anything small or subtle. It has to be grand, over the top. But he has a way of making every other gesture seem small. How am I going to go out there and be impressed?" She calls Stefan to thank him for the roses and tells him that she has friends visiting for the week. This buys her time.

Five days later he shows up in her office with two tickets to the Maldives, exotic coral islands off the coast of India. She has never even heard of them. He tells her that he wants to take her there as a belated birthday present. She stares up at his creased forehead and tries to think of what to say.

Every now and then, Casey seems to be arm wrestling with herself. One side of her sees Stefan as her anchor, the only real adult in her New York life, the one who is genuine and sure and there. The other side wants to hold out for something more, something that knocks the dead air out of her lungs.

She tells him that she needs to think about the trip and spends the rest of the day filing reports about her bands, stopping to stare out her window at the rows of midtown office buildings. When she gets home, she calls Stefan and tells him that she would love to go to the Maldives. Sometimes the something more can be a place, a peek into another world.

"I have another offer for you," he says after they talk about the dates for their trip. "How would you like to accompany me to the awards ceremony tomorrow night?"

Stefan and Casey have never been seen in public as a couple. She's always told colleagues that he was her mentor; he helped her land her first job. Rumors swirled around every so often, but Stefan squashed them by appearing out regularly with tamborine girls and exotic dancers. She told herself that she would never be one of his "ornaments." But she pulls on a black dress with skinny straps and meets him at his apartment the following night.

They arrive at the awards ceremony late, just behind one of Casey's old bosses. "Hello there," he says, grinning. It occurs to her that she has no explanation for why she is with Stefan. He lifts his chin at them, still grinning, as they head to their seats. After the ceremony, Stefan and Casey take a cab to a hotel suite for a post-awards party. The room is full of people Casey knows from work — managers and media and store reps. She is trying to introduce them to Stefan, but he is looking away. He excuses himself and disappears into a huddle of men in dark suits. She heads to the bar with Beth from work.

She stops to look over at him once, her idol, her adviser. He is bored with all this. She is just starting to enjoy it — her career. She knows everyone and she is taken seriously, but she is not too jaded to get a kick out of it.

Casey is still staring over at Stefan when she feels a hand on her back, then a dry, scratchy kiss on her cheek. She looks up to see one of her artists, the lead singer of a heavy-metal band. His voice is deep and parched and his hand shakes when he tries to light his cigarette. "Are you okay?" she asks him.

"Yeah, I'm just a little jet-lagged. We just got back from Asia."

"I'm heading near there myself next month," she says.

"Where to?"

"The Maldives."

"The Maldives? Sounds romantic. With who?"

"Oh, just an old friend."

The man exhales smoke up at the ceiling, then looks around the hotel suite.

"Listen," he says, leaning in. "Don't settle. You've got to hold out for the one who makes you *taste it*. You have to feel it with your weight, feel it right *here*." He punches his fist against his stomach.

This is the only detail from her week that Casey shares with her brother.

May

If you don't have good stories to tell on

your deathbed, what good was living?

—Sandra Bullock,

quoted in *Cosmo*

Jen

JEN IS BLUE. It's been almost three weeks since she visited New York, but she is still feeling sort of . . . hollow. It's not clear what's worse, realizing you can't have something or realizing you don't want it anymore. She is mourning the New York of her faraway imagination. This last trip really killed it. Now she is longing to long.

Her sister still worries that Jen will go back there. Jen always seems to be homesick. Actually, she is homesick, but it is no longer about a place. She is sick for something to feel like home. Becca does not completely understand. For her, home is where Alex is and, more and more these days, where Jen is. Becca's husband has been away a lot for work, and Jen has had to step in. "I am not your *pet!*" Jen yells into the receiver one guilt-laden Sunday. "I am not going to spend my Saturday nights with you."

The truth is, Jen is starting to feel more like the daughter her sister has yet to have. Sometimes she just wants to spend her Saturday nights home alone.

But when Becca's husband leaves for Toronto for the week, Jen agrees to go with her to Palm Springs for a long weekend — a three-day therapy camp. Palm Springs is, really, no place for a home-starved near-thirty single woman. There is too much white hair and white architecture. But there are also clothing outlets — serious outlets — and Becca is wise to the power of serious outlet shopping. She sends Jen into the dressing room of the Barney's outlet to try on a beaded camisole, and once she's out of sight, sneaks up to the cash register to buy two pairs of white pleated tennis skorts.

Sunday is tennis lesson day. When they were in middle school, they used to fight over a pair of Chris Evert skorts. Becca reveals her purchase—now they each have their own. Of course, the new whites bear the name of some Swiss girl half their age. They wake up early Sunday morning and pull their hair up into tight, high ponytails. Then they pull on their matching skorts and jog to the hotel courts.

"Is Brad going to be there?" Jen jokes, pressing her pleats with her palms. Brad was the dimpled, sweaty tennis coach at Newton Tennis Camp. Jen and Becca begged their parents for more tennis lessons with Brad. He used to show up in his white Izod tennis shorts and his tan, taut quadriceps.

The jogging comes to an abrupt halt when they spot Darrell, the hotel tennis pro. He's a dirty-blond Orange County surfer, wearing a lime-green tank top and droopy knee-length surf shorts. He has Luke Perry sideburns and a southern California drawl. This is what surfers without waves do, Jen thinks. They become Palm Springs hotel tennis pros.

Tennis isn't half as much fun as they remember, and after their lesson, they stare down at their little skorts. Becca pulls a small black camera out of her bag and takes a picture of Jen. The skorts will not be in vain! It is time for the next activity of therapy camp: deep tissue massage at the Givenchy Spa, the famous four-star pampering palace. Becca is treating Jen to this one. Her husband, Alex, is an entertainment lawyer and together they have a very nice combined income—and no kids to pamper yet. Inside the spa chambers, a large European man pummels Jen's back with his elbows while she surrenders small noises of pain.

After their massage, they hobble to the women's pools—the pools are divided by sex because no one is wearing clothes. It's not clear whether clothes are even allowed. The water is full of starved, blond, naked women over fifty, and Jen can't bring herself to unwrap her towel. She and Becca can't stop giggling.

"So, now what do we do? The whirlpool?" Becca asks.

"Eew," Jen says.

Becca finally drops her towel and dives quickly into the pool. Jen clings tighter to hers. Then she gets up and brisk-walks to the sauna room. "Puritan!" Becca yells, safely submerged in the pool.

On the drive home from Palm Springs, Becca launches into the final camp activity: talk therapy. "I think you should just have sex with Nate."

"What?" Jen has just finished explaining how Nate is going on vacation with a new woman.

"Have sex with him. Then you can move on."

"You just want me to have a one-night stand because you can't."

"Not true. I think it would be healthy. All Nate is at this point is something you can't have, so have him and be done with it. Not many people in this world can have guilt-free sex. You have to realize what's great about your life."

She has a point, Jen decides. The problem is, somewhere between twelve and sixteen, afraid her little sister would be labeled a sleaze, Becca raised Jen to be a puritan.

Anna

IT'S MAY, AND Ethan is on his way to San Francisco. He called Anna the day before he left Austin to tell her that he had finally ended things with the girlfriend, and he's driving up the coast to Portland to get away for a while. He asked if he could stay with her for two nights. She is still sunburned down to her collarbone from her ski trip—though Gwen insists that it's lingering sex flush. Whatever the case, she has lost her cowboy cravings. She does not even shave her legs for his visit.

Ethan shows up at her office in a denim shirt, jeans, and boots. She takes him for a quick office tour, introducing him to Jeanne and Lizzie and the assistants. She brings him upstairs to meet an important creative director, explaining all the work Ethan has done for her Austin campaign. Then she sends him up to the rec room with a nerf basketball while she finishes her work. "Why didn't you tell us he looked like *that?*" one of the assistants whispers loudly into her office.

On the way home from work, they stop at a Middle Eastern restaurant in her neighborhood. He orders pita bread with "hoomus," and the waiter stares at him, puzzled. "He means hummus," Anna explains. She is puzzled, too. What kind of Renaissance Cowboy orders "hoo-mus"? And why does she have a problem with this?

Dunking his pita bread into the pureed chickpeas, Ethan starts telling Anna about his girlfriend, Sophia. Things between them "got a little ugly" at the end, and he had to get out of town. His friends don't really understand him, and Anna's the only one he can be completely honest with. When they get back to her apartment, she tries not to sit too close to him. She talks rapidly about her ski trip and about her new client at work.

"What's wrong with you?" he finally asks.

She goes to the fridge and grabs two beers, then tells him about the guy she met in Colorado.

He is grimacing. "Why are you *doin'* this?" he says. (Anna likes to imitate Ethan's accent. Whenever she recounts his end of their conversations, she drops down a few octaves and adds a twang. " 'I've been having *fan*-ta-sies about you, *ba*by.' *Ba*by. That's a Tex-as bad-cow-boy *thang.*")

"Well, you've said that honesty is important," she tells him. "I'm just trying to be honest. I'm a little uncomfortable being with you right now."

Ethan spends the night on the couch. She listens to his heavy sighs for half an hour before she falls asleep. On her way out the door to work the next morning, she stares down at him for a minute and watches him sleep. He's curled up in a fetal crouch on her bumpy couch, limbs falling onto her coffee table.

She meets him at an Italian café in North Beach after work, and they share a bottle of wine. He apologizes for dropping in and dumping his problems on her. "Look, it's good that you've met someone else," he says. "But I just want us to enjoy each other's company." Then he offers to take her to dinner downtown at Bix, an old supper club she'd talked about once over the phone.

Most people go to Bix to sit in a banquette up on the balcony, but since they don't have a reservation, the hostess seats them downstairs at a small table next to an eerie-looking European couple. Halfway through dinner, the couple start talking to Anna and Ethan in thick accents. They are very friendly. Anna decides they must be on something. "I think they're trying to pick us up," Ethan whispers to Anna when the couple's waiter comes. "No!" she says, trying not to stare over at them. Ten minutes later she excuses herself to go to the bathroom, and the European woman follows her.

Anna pads her face in the bathroom mirror nervously while the woman washes her hands next to her. She looks up and smiles at Anna in the mirror. "That man you are weeth is ver-dy sex-see," she says. Anna nods her head slowly. "But he likesz you moch more than you like him."

"Oh, I don't know about that," Anna says to the woman, and quickly leaves the bathroom. Her hands are now shaking. She is trying to figure out if Ethan knows the woman, if he paid her to come in there and be weird. Back at their table, Anna stares carefully at the man sitting next to them, then over at Ethan. They could not possibly know each other. She flags the waiter and tells Ethan it's time to leave.

They head to a smoky pool bar in the Mission, order a pitcher of beer, and sign up for a pool game. He *is* sexy, she thinks staring over at him as he stares at his cue stick. He is a wanted man, a wanted bad cowboy, and he is with her.

Ten minutes later, he's intensely concentrating on his pool game, ignoring her. She leans over the pool table and tries to distract him, but it doesn't work. Then she announces that for every ball he sinks, she'll unbutton a button on her blouse. "I'm wearing this shirt with a thousand buttons, but I start working my way down. I can tell he thinks I won't do it." She stops three quarters of the way and buttons it back up.

Walking home, Anna starts talking about Henry, her gay friend from New York who's flying in to visit this weekend. "I'm drunk and I'm carrying on about how much fun I have with Henry. He gets annoyed. I tell him that Henry loves me very much. So he pins me up against this building and he says 'I'll show you I can love you in a way Henry can't,' and rips open my blouse right there on the street. It scared me. He did something I would never have done. He found that point of difference."

They spend the night together, this time in Anna's bed, and when she wakes up the next morning, she is completely unearthed. She almost faints on the way to the bathroom. She offers few details aside from this: "Okay, the difference between a twenty-five-year-old skier and a thirty-seven-year-old Ethan is — older men just know what they're doing. The twenty-five-year-old skier was like the little kid who sticks the whole Oreo into his mouth at once. Older men just know how to eat an Oreo. They've been trained, or they've been cut off, so they have to know what they're doing."

After he leaves, she spends the day sleeping. When she wakes up, at five o'clock that afternoon, she calls Gwen. "I will never have better sex in my whole life."

Casey

CASEY AND STEFAN have made it to their thatched-roof bungalow at a posh resort on a tiny green island in the Maldives. The flight over was long and dark, and now, from their terrace, they can see the pale-blue ocean beach ahead and an emerald lagoon through the trees. Their room has a wrought-iron bed, shrouded in muslin and surrounded by tall potted palms. On a table sit bowls of orange-yellow fruit and teas. The whole place smells of coconut.

It's two in the afternoon, their first day at the resort. Stefan has collapsed into a big chair with his airplane book, a biography of Andy Warhol. He doesn't really like the sun. He takes a break to order room service, then picks up his book again. Casey has been pacing around the room, stopping to flip through her guidebook. She changes into her black bikini and tells him she'll meet him on the beach.

She jogs across the white sand and doesn't pause when she reaches the ocean, running into the water until she is deep enough to swim, then dunking her head all the way back to soak her hair off her face. She starts sidestroking down the beach, stopping every five minutes to look for Stefan. When he doesn't appear, she kicks and splashes harder, slicing the water with her arms until she is out of breath. It's her first day in the most exotic place she has ever seen, and her date is inside, lost in some plastic-fantastic biography. She swims to shore at the resort's pavilion, signs out a big towel, and falls into a hammock.

A man in a white shirt approaches her, carrying a tray. He leans over her with a small towel and her arm jerks up to stop him. No one has ever presumed to dab her brow before.

"I'm sorry, Mrs. Van der Beer," the man says, using Stefan's name. "May I get you a drink?"

"It's Ms. Barr," she says, startled. "I'll have an orange juice, please," she adds, trying to sound casual. Casey looks around the beach. She is surrounded by honeymooners, giggling couples, women who would be thrilled to be called Mrs. Van der Beer. She turns herself around to face the ocean.

That night the place cards at their table say Mr. Van der Beer and Miss Barr. Casey smiles at Stefan. He is already lost in his menu. Back in their bungalow after dinner, he lies down in their bed and picks up his book. Already tan from her first day on the beach, Casey puts on a gauzy white halter dress. Stefan likes gauzy dresses and slinky lingerie. For his birthday people give him soft-porn books. "He's snuck these thoughts into my hippie world," she says. "When I'm around him, I somehow slip into this role — I'm his little vamp out of the lingerie catalog."

Casey flips her hair over and combs it upside down, then stretches across the king-sized bed and props herself up on an elbow. Stefan scratches his stomach, reaches over to pet her hair, and turns another page of his book.

She rolls over onto her back and sighs. Then she gets up and heads for the terrace. He joins her a half-hour later and pulls her back inside.

"If I had known that was going to be pretty much the only sex we would have all week, I would have taken better notes," she reports. "I think it was standard Stefan. Sex with him is very clinical. He's like a doctor. He's watched a lot of sex videos. Very skilled, but in a way that is sort of distracting. I'm always thinking, 'Where has this guy *been*?' And in the middle of it, there's this 'Oh, yeah, I'm supposed to be kissing you while we do this.'

"But I kind of surrendered to it. I used to be very uptight around him. I was very 'You must respect me for my business prowess.' But now I can sort of let go."

It took Casey a long time to let go. When she was five and people would ask her what she wanted to be when she grew up, she would say "a leader." At ten, she changed her answer to "Olympic athlete." At sixteen, she just wanted to stay out all night. She was back in the states, trying to fit in. She would sneak into bars with her new friends and watch the local bands play cover songs of REO Speedwagon. She remembers watching the band's girlfriends on the side of the stage, dragging on their cigarettes and pulling at their leotards. Then one night, after a Rush cover band stopped playing, she watched the lead singer push his girlfriend away to talk to a band booker. That's when she decided she wanted to be on the business side of the industry.

"I didn't want to be just another girl fan," she explains. "And I guess I could no longer compete with guys on the soccer field, so I had to get them to respect me for something else."

Now Casey has lots of something elses, but it doesn't seem to make a difference this weekend.

The next morning she gets up early and makes a list of adventures. Snorkeling on the coral reef. Sailing a catamaran to the other islands. Skinny-dipping under the moon at midnight. Figuring out the Southern Cross. She runs her list by Stefan. This time he is scratching his chest hair. "My knee is really bothering me today," he tells her. He finally agrees to join her snorkeling after he hears her making a reservation for one. When they get back to their room several hours later, he's asleep inside ten minutes.

She stares over at him, then out at the other bungalows. They are not even married and already they have stopped having sex. She pulls out her guidebook and starts to read about the island's history. Then she starts thinking about Bruce. She and Bruce would have sex in the middle of breakfast. He would wrestle her all over their living room floor.

She looks over at Stefan and tries to imagine him rolling around with her on the floor. Stefan was raised by European aristocrats. He thinks wrestling is childish.

Back in New York, it was Casey who was trying not to have sex with Stefan. She had a lot on her mind—her breakup with Bruce, work, cameramen. And Stefan was away so often that they had lost any momentum. But now she is in the Maldives, in a Brooke Shields movie set, and she is tanned and toned and bored. People take twenty-hour flights to the Maldives just to have steamy sex. Stefan is snoring like a horse.

The following morning, she wakes up early and signs up for a massage. Her back is in knots from all of the water thrashing. A silver-haired Indian woman begins kneading her spine. "You have very nice body," the woman says, pushing her elbows into Casey's shoulder blades. Casey laughs into her pillow. She charges the massage to Stefan's bill and gives the woman a big tip.

Over breakfast after her massage, Stefan puts down his paper and studies the menu. "This place is not as good as it used to be." *Used to* be? Stefan finally confesses that he's been to the Maldives before. After some prying, actually a solid minute of silent staring, Casey learns that he brought his wife to the same resort just a few years ago. Casey tries to picture her for a minute—nails meticulously manicured, lying motionless by the pool, waiting for the forehead dabber. This was probably her idea of the perfect vacation—free from movement or interaction.

They hardly speak during the entire flight back. Alone in her apartment the first night home, Casey drops her bags by the door, crawls into bed, and calls her brother.

"I felt as if I'd been married for years, Brett."

"Case."

"What?"

"He *is* married."

"His divorce is almost final," she drifts off for a minute. "Did he just conquer me?" she says after a long pause. "Did I become his wife by agreeing to go on this trip with him?"

"It did sound kind of like a honeymoon."

"We had sex about three times all week. What kind of honeymoon is that?"

"Probably two times more than on his real honeymoon. Maybe he's depressed."

"If you could have seen this place, there's no way anyone could be depressed there. I think he just decided that he was spending money on me, so he could settle back into his selfish, stuffy self." Casey sighs.

"Maybe he felt guilty about his wife."

"Ex-wife. Brett, the guy has been dating exotic dancers for the last three years. He's had plenty of time to feel guilty. All I know is I would have been less lonely if I had gone alone."

Jen

IT'S SUNDAY, IN the middle of May, and Jen is feeling better. Becca's therapy camp did the trick. And after three days in Palm Springs, L.A. feels better—young, ocean-cooled, colorful. And her *Los Angeles Times* "week ahead" horoscope says that she will be reunited with an old flame out of the blue. She has been blue! They got this right. And she has a whole week to wait for the reunion. She gets a sudden pang of sadness for her sister. Becca probably doesn't even read her horoscope anymore. What would be the point? "This week you will spend five more nights with the same man, and you already know damn well who he is."

She arrives at work Monday morning to find a message from her assistant. "Griffin Eaton called you." Griffin is the Luke Skywalker look-alike who works for one of the bigwigs upstairs. They met in front of their company's parking lot two months ago. He had Massachusetts license plates, and they talked about growing up in Boston. The following week, she had E-mailed him a cute, non-threatening invitation to see a "hometown band only a Bostonian will love." He sent back a "Sounds great!" and told her he would meet her there.

Two days and a sixty-dollar camisole later, she'd sat watching the hometown band with Emily. At midnight, alone with her drink, she finally left. A week passed before she got his second E-mail: "Hey, sorry I missed the band. Some other time." And then she got a phone call: "Would you like to have lunch?" It was Mr. No-show's boss. She didn't pause before saying yes. "I told him I would meet him in the foyer, just outside Luke-alike's office," she recalls gleefully. "These are rules you can't get from a book."

Her lunch date was a turning point. For the first time, she caught herself admiring the cut of a sharp suit and the hold of a good gob of hair gel. Indignation has a way of opening the mind.

Jen hasn't spoken to Griffin since. He sits near her in staff meetings and occasionally looks over, but he never even musters a hello. She has flashbacks to seventh-grade assemblies, sometimes to fourth-grade fire drills. She decides not to call him back. But then she thinks: He is sort of an old crush. Can you be reunited with an old flame who works downstairs and that never quite ignited? She braces herself for his apology and pushes the buttons on her phone.

"Oh, hey," he says. "Listen, I heard you mention that project in last week's staff meeting. I think I've got the perfect actress for you."

"Actually, it's already done. We finished casting."

"Well, you weren't here yesterday, so I mentioned it to Harry. He seemed into it, so I sent over some tapes."

"Well, Harry's got a lot of other things on his plate. He probably thought you were talking about the teenage thriller project." Not even a slow-dying ash.

"Uh, he seemed to know what I was talking about. I think Rick has been gunning for this one. Anyway, I'll just send this stuff over to you. I think there's a fit."

Jen yanks her headset out of its socket. "Fucking little self-promoting *weasel*." It's all she can do not to spit into her phone base.

The next day, Jen gets a call from Justin Grimaldi. Justin is an old . . . ember. More like a half-lit charcoal briquette. They were dancing one late night at the Pleasure Palace two years ago, a sort of freestyle ballroom performance, and they started kissing. That was pretty much the end of it, but since everyone witnessed the encounter, and since Justin rarely even socializes, she has had a little trouble living it down. There is also the detail that Justin was Max the guitarist's college roommate. Convenient if not intentional.

Justin is sort of shy, socially pained, actually, but he has had some success as an independent filmmaker in recent years. In fact, he's in L.A. to meet an agent, and he'd love to meet Jen if she is free. Aside from that night at the Palace, Jen doesn't remember ever speaking to Justin.

Over drinks at the Hollywood Spin, Justin turns out to be charming. He's been living in Chicago with his family, building an addition to their house and writing scripts. He is the farthest thing from a Hollywood guy. He has trouble making eye contact, much less pawing Jen's arms. "I'm so reclusive that if I don't put myself around people soon, I may never speak to anyone again," Justin says into his beer.

Justin brings up Keith, their friend who just came out of the closet. Jen isn't sure if Justin knows yet. Justin is sort of old-world Italian straight, a super Y-chromosome guy, so straight he is afraid of girls.

"I met Keith's new man," he says, eyebrows hiked.

"Isn't he a prince?" Jen blurts out.

"He really is. I got really drunk and I told Keith that after meeting Jay I've started to question my own sexuality. I'll never meet a woman half as perfect."

"You won't," Jen says, staring out the window.

The evening ends with the shuffling of feet and an awkward wave good-bye, both of them looking away.

Friday holds the last chance for the *L.A. Times* weekly horoscope prediction to come through. Justin barely counts as a former flame, and last night was hardly a reunion, but Jen is ready to talk herself into anything. Sitting at her desk Friday morning, she pictures Justin, head drooping, eyes blinking, like an Old English sheepdog. She *loved The Shaggy D.A.*

The Justin-as-flame story line is unfolding in her head when she gets a phone call.

"What are you wearing?" a low voice says.

"Uh . . . my headset?" She recognizes the big laugh. "Sir James?"

"I thought you'd think I was a big Hollywood agent."

"Or my boss."

"Really? So where's your assistant, out getting your dry cleaning?"

"Actually, she's out getting my frappacinos."

"That is so cool. What's it like to wield so much power over the little people?"

James is the blond from the Indie Awards. He has long, crinkly yellow hair, the color of . . . *flames!* He must be the man from the *L.A. Times* horoscope. She agrees to have dinner with him the following week.

Anna

ANNA IS SITTING at home watching the news. The U.S. economy is enjoying the best times in twenty-five years. It's boom time in America. She is supposed to be having the greatest time since first grade.

Over three weeks have passed since Anna heard from Ethan. He called in early May to tell her that he was leaving for Costa Rica with Sophia, his "ex"-girlfriend. They had planned the trip a long time ago, he told Anna, and they couldn't get a refund for the tickets.

As soon as he told her this, she dug through her old date book for the number of the therapist she saw when she first moved to San Francisco, the one with middle-parted Gloria Steinem hair. How could she have lulled herself back into this state? She booked a therapy session, then called to report that she was actually relieved. Her state had been one of suspension; she is no longer sure how to process him. Is it strictly physical? Chemical? Emotional? How is she supposed to know the difference? At least this trip will force a resolution. "Either they will kill each other off down there or they will end up together. But it will be resolved."

She finally calls him on his birthday, the day the television informs her of the good times. She knows he's got to be back from the vacation. "What's going on with *you*?" she asks after filing the update on her life.

"Well, things are kind of crazy around here. We, uh, got some news."

"Oh. We?"

"You're going to be mad at me," he says.

She pauses for a few seconds, bracing herself for honesty. "You ate all of mommie's cookies?" she says anxiously.

"Sophia's pregnant."

She pulls the phone away from her face for a moment. "You dirty dog," she finally says into the receiver. She pictures herself, eyes glazed over, a stuffed caribou greeting hunters at the bullet convention.

It turns out that Sophia was pregnant before their trip, maybe even before Ethan visited Anna in San Francisco. She's very Italian and very Catholic, he explains calmly. She is going to have the baby. But they've decided they are not getting married. According to Ethan, Sophia doesn't want to get married. She is a special kind of "very Catholic," the unmarried-mother kind.

"You dirty dog," Anna repeats. "Nice job. I could not have se-
lected a better partner for you."

"I'm trying, babe. I'm trying to do something right this time."

"HONESTY IS HIGHLY overrated," Anna says later. "I'm sick of
being burdened with too much knowledge about this guy."

After the phone call, she leaves her apartment and takes a bus
to the animal shelter she passes every day on her way to work. A
somber tiger cat with dark stripes stares up at her from his cage
with a scowl. He seems to be mimicking her. She takes him home
and names him Dan. "As in Rather. He's very serious — never cracks
a smile."

The next day, she visits the long-haired therapist. Lizzie's sister
recommended this person last year when Anna was having second
thoughts about her divorce from Greg, but Anna quickly ended the
visits. "It was a little too California for me. Lots of inner-child stuff.
I wanted the Woody Allen treatment."

Now she just needs someone to feel sorry for her, and she is
willing to pay for professional pity. When she is finished telling the
tale of the bad cowboy, the bad Catholic, and the baby, the therapist closes her eyes. "I'm just trying to imagine what little Anna
must be feeling," she says after a long sigh. "Would you let little
Anna care about this man?"

"No," Anna sniffles. "But then I would be a sane person and I
wouldn't be on your couch right now."

The therapist blinks slowly and smiles. Anna tries again.

"I'd get little Anna the hell away from him. And his cowboy
boots."

The woman offers Anna some Kleenex and a protruded lower lip.

"But if he really loved her, they'd be married, right?" Anna says
in a small voice.

The therapist scowls.

The next day Anna goes to work and calls Lizzie into her office.
"Are you ready for this one?" There is one boon to the Ethan story:
Anna gets to tell Lizzie. She has been looking forward to telling

Lizzie the news all weekend. "You are going to be floored," she tells her. Lizzie sits down on the edge of a chair and waits eagerly for the story. This one is going to be good.

"Wow," is all Lizzie can say at first. She never guessed it would be *that* good. She covers her mouth to stop her nervous giggles, and pretty soon they're both huddled over, wheezing again. When they named him "bad cowboy," it was supposed to be as in "bad actor," as in *not quite*. They didn't plan on him turning into a Willie Nelson song.

Lizzie runs out of Anna's office and returns two minutes later with a framed photograph of Ronald Reagan. He's dressed in a two-tone western shirt with curvy arrows, leather chaps, and a ten-gallon hat. Underneath the photo it says "American Cowboy." Lizzie crosses out "American" and writes in "Bad." She puts the photograph on Anna's desk.

Two days later, Dan Rather jumps out the window of her apartment and crushes his pelvis. Anna heard a screeching meow as she was getting dressed for work and ran to the open window. "I was playing Madonna, the *Immaculate Collection* CD. I think he hates Madonna. But he didn't have to attempt suicide." Anna couldn't find a ride to the cat hospital, so she had to take him, screaming, on the bus. The vet managed to patch him up. It cost her fifteen hundred dollars.

It costs about seven thousand dollars to give birth. Dan Rather is a bargain.

June

Our mothers didn't expect to find the moon
and stars in another human being, or to
perfect the institution of marriage. My
parents had the good sense not to look for
so much *from* each other that they couldn't
stick *with* each other.

—Margaret Carlson,

Time magazine

Casey

THE TRIP TO the Maldives was a big letdown, and now Casey is back at work, throwing herself into the details—making phone calls, setting up appointments, filling up the pages of her planner. There is no time to sit still, and no time to think. For as long as she can remember, she has had layers of people to keep her from having to question things. There was the man she was seeing, and the man she would think about when the man she was seeing let her down. Right now, all she has is paper, layers of message slips and record reports and planner pages.

The good news is that throwing herself into work means focusing on the weekend's Tibetan Freedom concert. On top of the eight hours she spends at her desk each day, Casey gets paid to watch live music, drink free drinks, and flirt with long-haired men. One of the young British bands on her company's label is in town for the concert, and Casey has booked a couple of interviews for the musicians. The concert is being held outside on Randalls Island, a wedge of abandoned land in the middle of the East River in upper Manhattan. It's the second year of the concert, and they are expecting over 100,000 fans to see a string of big acts like U2 and Pearl Jam and the Beastie Boys. Casey's friend Margot is in town from Chicago, and she has invited Margot to come along.

When they arrive at the central concert stage, several monks dressed in red and saffron robes are kicking off the concert with a speech of gratitude, followed by a Buddhist chant. Several of the audience members hum in unison. It sounds like "om," the Buddhist word for the universal sound of the universe, also the name of a new Gap fragrance. Other audience members start chanting "*Beas-tie Boys.*" They're the younger crowd, and they're not entirely sure what's going on. The first band takes the stage, and as the musicians tune their instruments, the lead singer gives a speech about China's violations of human rights in Tibet. The kids quiet down a little.

Throughout the day, monks and musicians take turns onstage, giving quiet speeches, playing loud songs. People are spread out on blankets and tapestries, or they are wandering around the grounds, eating Tibetan food and buying Gypsy jewelery from the vendors. There are a few white "monastery" tents for people who want to sit and meditate.

Buddhism has become the hot religion, according to the news-weeklies, and everyone has a theory why—its nonviolent message in a violent time, its therapeutic focus on the self and "well-being," and the charismatic appeal of the Dalai Lama. "Prophets always said that toward the end of the millennium, people would start to wake up," Casey offers. And this makes sense: the year 2000 looms in the not-so-far-off distance like a gigantic thirtieth birthday. Everyone is panicking, taking stock, soul-searching.

Casey was ahead of her time. She was introduced to Buddhism by her first New York roommate twelve years ago. The woman chanted every morning in their living room. "It freaked me out a little at first. But it was a focus thing for her. It was a form of Buddhism based on the idea that if you focus on what you desire, you can make it happen. It was the end of the eighties, and my roommate's friends would chant about getting a car. It just seemed incredibly materialistic to me. It was as if they had joined a cheer-leader cult, a sorority, only with chanting."

Still, Casey liked the idea of "focusing." It was through her room-mate that she became interested in yoga and meditation, and she is open to other people's rituals. "You can get really wound up living here. Everyone needs something to believe in. I don't know what I would be like if I didn't have yoga to calm me down."

Casey has other theories about why Tibetan Buddhism is so pop-ular today. "It's a lot more personal and more practical than other religions because it starts with you. *You* are responsible for your own happiness; you're not just waiting for something or someone to save you. You've got to figure it out for yourself first, and if you can do that, you can be compassionate about other people." She also likes the idea that, in a city as mixed as New York, it's a way to relate to people who grew up with different religions. "You don't have to reject what you come from to adopt it, because it's really just a very basic philosophy."

At four in the afternoon, Casey heads backstage to look for her musicians. They are scheduled to play in an hour, and they were told to show up early for an interview with a British magazine. She leaves her friend Margot in the beer tent with a radio producer and heads backstage to see if her band is okay.

"Groovy shirt, Reuben!" she says when she sees one of her musicians holding drumsticks. "I brought you echinacea."

"Where's my pot?" he asks.

"Not until you finish your interview," she says, turning away. "Hey, Slam, your album sold ten thousand pieces this week," she says to a guy in a fisherman's hat.

"Bloody hell, I didn't know that."

"What does that mean?" the guy with drumsticks asks.

"It means you're climbing the charts with a bullet!" Casey yells from a hallway.

She runs back out to the grounds to find the media tent and look for the British reporter. When she doesn't find him, she stops at a food vendor and buys a cardboard box full of Tibetan food. Her band boys will have the munchies soon. A young girl in a ponytail and brown lipstick stops her as she squeezes by the sawhorses behind the stage. "Will you take this to the bassist?" she asks, pressing a note into Casey's palm. "Of course," Casey says smiling. As she's ducking behind the sawhorses, she realizes that the girl meant the one already onstage. She hands the note off, like a baton, to the group's manager backstage. He is used to these relays.

Casey's band plays to a packed crowd, and after the musicians finish their interviews, Casey and Margot head back to the beer tent. On their way, they stop off to check out a monastery tent. Margot takes Casey's lead and sits cross-legged on a mat behind a row of monks. Twenty minutes later, they are both asleep on their mats. When they wake up, they head to the buses and ride back into the harried city.

The Sunday night after the two-day concert, Casey takes Margot to the wrap party in lower Manhattan. They get dressed up at her apartment: tight bootleg Levi's, clingy black tops, black slides. Margot starts to dab Casey's patchouli oil on her neck. "Whoa," Casey says, stopping her. "I have rules about patchouli oil. It's an aphrodisiac, so you can't abuse it." Casey's bohemian tastes have their boundaries. She offers Margot her Chanel bottle and swabs some on herself.

They take a cab to an abandoned jazz club in the twenties. It's the kind of place you have to know to find. There is a security guard in front, but he just smiles at Casey and Margot as they pull open the dark door. Once inside, they go straight to the bar and order vodkas. They survey the room from the bar platform. It's a serious crowd, and there are lots of tiny eyeglasses. It is also an exclusive event, which means there is no need for a VIP room. The musicians mingle with the handlers, sitting underneath long mirrors in elevated booths.

"There is a camaraderie here that comes with pulling off a special event," Casey explains. "It's not usually like this."

Margot is looking around the club. Everyone is pink-faced and delirious from being out in the sun for two days. She stops to stare at someone across the room. "There's a man over there checking you out," she whispers to Casey. Casey raises her eyebrows and tries not to turn around.

"Let me guess—the Edge?" she smirks. She shifts her weight and tucks her shirt in nervously, then turns around. The man is Stefan, and he is staring at her butt. She rolls her eyes and lowers her head to catch his line of vision. His eyes narrow, then widen with recognition.

"Oh, hello!" he says approaching them. He is swaying, a glass of scotch in his hand. "I didn't know you were coming." He tries to give her a wet kiss on the mouth, but she turns and offers her cheek.

"This is my friend Margot. She's visiting from Chicago."

"Hello," Margot says, politely holding out her hand. Stefan pulls lightly on her fingers, then lets go.

"What did you think of the festival?" he asks.

"Oh, I thought it was really interesting." Margot has just spotted a very familiar man behind Stefan, and he is turning around to see what she is distracted by.

"Oh, *fuck* Michael Stipe," he says, turning back to his scotch.

Casey cringes. Behind Michael Stipe is her boss. She excuses herself and goes to the bathroom, leaving Margot alone with Stefan. She lingers at the bathroom sink for five minutes too long, blotting her face. She doesn't want to spend the rest of her night with him leaning on her, picking fights. She waits until he is distracted, talking to someone else, and then she rescues Margot.

"I think we're going to head," she says to him on their way out.

"Don't tell me that's *the* Stefan," Margot says as they try to hail a cab on Fifth Avenue.

"I'm afraid it was. You got to see him in all his flying colors."

"What a shame. That party seemed like so much fun. What was with that handshake? They don't shake like that in Chicago."

In the cab on the way back to her apartment, Casey tries to remember how she must have described him to Margot, how she must have described him to herself. Who can she blame for how disappointed she feels?

And maybe this is another part of the appeal of Buddhism. Unlike Stefan, the Dalai Lama could never really let you down.

Jen

ACCORDING TO THE *L.A. Times,* unemployment is the lowest it's been in a generation. Jen has been thinking about asking for a raise. Then again, if it hadn't been for the *L.A. Times* and that ridiculous horoscope, she would not be in such a bad mood right now.

She is late for her date with James, the ponytailed screenwriter. Actually, she's not sure what he does for a living. All she remembers are the Converse sneakers and his Muhammad Ali song. And when she remembers this, she can't remember why she agreed to go on this date.

Still, she has dressed with expectation: her mother's black linen halter top from the sixties and white ankle-cut jeans. Her hair is pulled up into a swoop. She can't find her car keys.

Outside, a small freckled boy is standing in her driveway, pointing at her window and mumbling about kitty cats. Running up behind him is a sharp-jawed man in a red plaid shirt.

"Yoda!" the boy yells when he sees a cat appear in Jen's living room window. The man starts laughing.

"We're kind of into *Star Wars* these days," he says brushing salty black hair off to the side. The movie was just re-released for its twentieth anniversary. Two decades ago, Jen was wearing Princess Leia loop braids, carrying around a McDonald's Yoda doll. "What's the kitty's name?" the man asks grinning.

"Rudy."

"Yody!" the little boy yells. "Pss, pss, pss."

The tall man stares through Jen's window into her living room. "That's a beautiful couch you have."

"Oh, thanks," Jen beams, sticking her fingers into her back pockets. "I got it, um, in Santa Monica."

"So, are you new to the street?"

It turns out the man is a furniture designer. He's been renting Jen's favorite house down the block. Jen lives in a tiny one-bedroom house — twelve hundred dollars a month — in Laurel Canyon, on a winding street with million-dollar bungalows. One of those bungalows belongs to this man.

"Lady, how old are you?" the little boy asks.

"Charlie! We don't ask people how old they are."

"Can I come inside and see your kitty cats? I want to hold your kitty cats." They watch as Rudy and Mamie squirm away into their cat treehouse. They are brother and sister indoor cats, a little rambunctious, and Jen adopted them when she first moved to L.A.

"My house is a cute little cat house," Jen says to the boy.

"My house is small too," the father responds. "But it's just nice when the kids come and visit."

Jen smiles at her feet and gets into her car, a black Volvo wagon. "Come back and see the kitties," she says to them as they head down the street.

At the Negril restaurant, she spots the yellow ponytail by the bar surrounded by a halo of smoke. Her date is cornering an agent in glasses. He has a pack of Marlboro Reds wedged between two fingers, a scotch between two more. He's taller than she remembers.

Over dinner, he orders jerk chicken raviolis—flat pasta over-stuffed with spicy shredded chicken. He is telling her about the acting he did in college, and thin strands of chicken are slithering into his mouth. Then he talks about the athlete's-foot-powder commercial he auditioned for. His sitcom pilot idea. And his film short. He finishes his ravioli, then he starts to laugh.

"I'm such a cliché" he chuckles. Jen laughs harder. "When did I become such an L.A. cliché?" Somewhere after the fungus audition and before the pilot, she thinks to herself. So much for record unemployment. All she meets are out-of-work L.A. clichés.

She smiles back at him and stares at the chicken shreds on his plate. At least he has a sense of humor about himself. She feels a little bad when he grabs the check and pays for dinner, so when the valet pulls up with her car, she gives him a long kiss good-bye.

Driving up her street, she nicks a mailbox trying to peer into the furniture man's house. She thought she saw a tuft of graying hair on a perfectly crafted couch. She inspects the damage to her car in her driveway, then heads inside and slumps down on the couch. Rudy and Mamie fight for a spot on her chest, a battle of competing purrs, kneading paws, and whiskers. "Why can't I find someone half as fun as you guys to curl up with?" she says, reaching for the remote. The light on her message machine is blinking once. It can only be her sister. She is debating whether to press "play" when the phone rings.

"How did it go?" Becca says as soon as Jen presses the "talk" button on her portable phone.

"Do you have my house bugged?"

"No. I just knew you'd be home by ten."

"I looked at my watch at eight-thirty."

"You're horrible! What could possibly be wrong with him?"

"Nothing," Jen sighs.

"I'm sure he has plenty of things wrong with him. Just give him another chance."

"I'm really not looking for another case. I'm just looking for someone . . . I have chemistry with."

"You are looking for Ralph Fiennes, someone *everyone* thinks they have chemistry with. You've got to give it another chance." Becca's voice is pleading. *Stay in L.A.*, she is really saying.

"I'm looking for Rudy and Mamie. *Hello, babies.* Maybe I'll take those ginseng aphrodisiacs and go out with him again."

"Yeah. Go get yourself some chemistry at the Vitamin Shoppe."

Jen decides Becca is right. She'll simply jack herself up with ginseng tablets and take the ponytail man out dancing. A few throbbing colored lights might help.

A half-hour later, the phone rings again. "*What?*" Jen snaps, certain it's her sister.

"I knew you'd be back for *Saturday Night Live.*"

It's Nate, and she's caught. She was planning to tell him she had a really big night with the ponytail.

"I ate this disgusting chicken ravioli and got sick. We were actually on our way to Spaceland. I had to turn off." Spaceland is where Nate goes to see all the new bands.

"Well, if it's any consolation, I'm home too, and I feel fine. Want to go get pizza?"

Jen had made a pact with herself that she would avoid Nate for a month. Lately he can't stop talking about his new woman back in New York. She plays some kind of instrument in a band, probably the maracas, and Nate calls her his "rock goddess."

"It's pathetic, really. He's infatuated with the up-onstage thing," she explains later.

"I thought your rock goddess was coming to town?" Jen says to Nate.

"Not until the Fourth." Nate's voice drifts off. She is picturing him reaching for some Kafka book. Jen has drifted off too. She is watching Norm McDonald deliver the fake news.

"I don't have anything to say to Tasha," Nate says after a long pause.

"That's because it's long-distance," Jen says, trying to be big. Really, she thinks, it's because you're her *groupie*. Then she pictures Lynn's annoyed smile, the night she left to go see Max play.

"I'm sure it will be fine when you see her."

"Mm. I just don't know."

"Nate," Jen says after another long pause. "I've got to go."

IT'S THE END of June, and adultery is in the news again. This time, an air force general's nomination for the top Pentagon job was withdrawn because he had an affair several years ago when he was separated from his wife.

One of the things Anna likes about being single is that no one is allowed to care whom she has affairs with. No one, that is, except her married friends.

"What the hell were you thinking?" Gwen yells into the phone. Anna has called her from Austin and announced that she slept with the bad cowboy again. She met him for drinks after her latest client meeting. "Are you trying to get pregnant too?"

"Don't be ridiculous."

"Where was the pregnant wife?" Gwen's voice is a mix of alarm and prurience.

"They're not getting married. They're not even sure they're going to stay together."

"Where was she?"

"She's back in Italy. Look, I had to do it. Whether anyone got it but me, I had to make it this purely physical thing. Prove that I wasn't in love with him — it was just this attraction to this opposite. It was one of the best things I've ever done."

"You are deluding yourself."

"No, I don't think I am. I always drag my heart into the bedroom, even when I'm just trying to . . . live a little, take advantage of my life."

Gwen sighs into the phone. Then she starts chewing in Anna's ear. She chews carrots when she is nervous. She's home in Philly, and she tells Anna she has to shut the door to her bedroom. "That's because you're a she," she says after two more sighs. "And shes are supposed to feel bad about it. We get ashamed if we don't have lots of feelings, and so we make them up."

"Well, exactly," Anna says, and pauses. "I had to show myself I made most of it up. When did I decide I was in love him? After I slept with him, and he gave me that speech about pushing me away. All of a sudden I'm being pushed away, and I feel bad, so I think I'm in love."

"Anna?"

"Yeah?"

"I think we're competing for emotional dysfunction."

"I know. But, you know, everybody's parents were emotionally unavailable at some point. We're all equally entitled to emotional dwarfhood."

"Just promise me you won't get pregnant."

Anna tells Gwen not to worry. The world doesn't need any more bad cowboys.

July

What many of us want is a marriage that doesn't seem to exist—a sexy friendship with somebody really funny who doesn't sleep over every night.

—Marcelle Clements,

author of *The Improvised Woman*

Casey

IT'S THE FOURTH of July weekend. The stock market is at a record high, the U.S. economy is booming, and the U.S. spacecraft *Pathfinder* and its rover *Sojourner* have just landed on Mars—the first Mars landing in two decades. So much patriotism and prosperity and possibility; it feels like the fifties.

Casey's spending the weekend in Atlanta to help with a live shoot of a heavy-metal concert. She'd convinced her boss to send her last week. After Margot and the British bands left town, she was back at her desk again, making calls, filing reports, setting up appointments. She decided she needed to get away, go on her own pathfinding mission. So she made a case to her boss that she should go to Atlanta for the concert to make sure they would get media-ready concert footage. The lead singer knows her; they made a connection a few months ago. She wants to make sure everything goes smoothly.

As soon as Atlanta was booked, Stefan called to apologize for his behavior at the Tibetan wrap party. He has not been himself lately—the divorce, work, traveling. He invited her to be his date at a big dinner in Los Angeles the following weekend. Her West Coast bosses will be there, he told her. She has been thinking about moving to L.A. lately. She needs a new landscape, new challenges, tanned hippies in cutoffs who get her. She tells Stefan she will think about it.

Meanwhile, she has hired a local freelance video director to handle the concert shoot in Atlanta. She arrives at the Fox Theatre soundstage and finds a lank, dark-eyed man in small frameless glasses sitting behind a sound-engineering board. His name is Leo, and he's preoccupied, talking into a microphone and sliding levers up and down. He barely notices her.

The concert is filling up with "headbangers," fourteen-year-olds in black T-shirts and bad haircuts. There are also lots of football player types, thrusting their big heads forward to the music.

Casey's not a big fan of this music, and she feels a little old. But having spent a few of her high school years in the Midwest, she understands the appeal. "It's an outlet for these kids. It's aggressive without being violent, like extreme sports. It gives people who don't have a lot of stimulation in their lives an adrenaline rush — without having to do drugs. And it's very physical, wailing on guitars, which is why all the jocks love it."

A half-hour before the concert begins, Leo — who was clearly a passive bookworm type in high school — asks Casey to sit with him and run through the lineup. He clears a seat next to him at the sound-engineer board, a large grid with hundreds of colored levers and lights. In a soft voice he starts to explain the important ones to her. When the lights go down, she begins whispering cues.

"There's a drum solo coming up here," she says.

He tilts his head toward hers, then slides two levers down and presses his mouth against a microphone: "Camera one," he says, taking her hands and placing them on a row of levers. "When I say so, shift them up," he whispers.

Casey grins. She has always wanted to do this. She is in the trenches, hand on the throttles, her chair vibrating with bass. In front of them, fifteen-year-olds are being hoisted over the crowds. She touches his shoulder and points to one heading straight for one of the cameras. "Camera two, heads up," Leo says into his mike. "Bodysurfer." She whispers another cue, and he nods. "You're up," he says to her.

After the shoot, the video crew meets for a drink at a local bar. Away from his levers, Leo withdraws into a corner. But the cameramen swarm in around Casey. She is the guest of honor. She can't stop grinning. She buys everyone a round of drinks.

"How did you like that?" one of the cameramen asks her.

"I loved it!" Casey says, looking at Leo. "Levers and cameras and lights. So much more fun than kissing band butt."

After an hour of crew talk, she approaches Leo and asks if he knows where the Hilton is. "It's on my way," he says quietly. "I'll lead you there."

She follows him through the city in her shiny rented car, blasting the radio, hitting the seek button, trying not to sing. She feels as if she's sixteen. She wants to go for a midnight swim in the pool. If she couldn't get Stefan to go for a swim under the moon in the Maldives, she will have Leo at the Atlanta Hilton.

When they pull up to the hotel, Casey is suddenly struck with a case of the dreads: What will he wear in the pool? And what if he says no? That would be awful. "My hotel has this great pool," she says as quickly as possible. "Do you want to go for a swim?"

He looks straight ahead and leans forward to fidget with something on his radio. Casey freezes. She pictures herself, hands on her hips, a towering record dominatrix, this timid man preparing to peel out. Then he pulls a gym bag out from in front of his passenger seat and fishes around inside it. She runs up to her room and slides on her high-cut one-piece. When she finds him at the pool, he is wearing nylon soccer shorts. Stefan would never have had a pair of nylon soccer shorts.

Glancing down at her naked legs, Casey feels slightly awkward. He's shy, and this is making her shy. They both dive into the flood-lit pool, swim to the other end, and jump out. The water has cooled. Casey sits on a chaise lounge, shivering, until he suggests that they both change.

Back in her room, they take turns using the bathroom to change back into jeans and T-shirts. Then she sits next to him on the couch. They talk nervously about music, drum solos, *Billboard* charts, colored lights. They are not really making any sense. After a half-hour, Casey gets up to go to the bathroom again, and when she returns, she sits closer to him. His back seems to stiffen. She has lost her nerve again.

"I have to get up early and fly to L.A. tomorrow," she says, rubbing her legs. "I should probably get some sleep."

Silence.

"I don't want to go," he finally answers, staring down at her feet. Then he turns abruptly and kisses her.

"He was completely transformed into this magnet man," Casey recalls. "I could not have peeled him off me."

In her journal, Casey called it "the night of a thousand kisses." The man was heavily into erogenous zones. He found erogenous zones she didn't even know she had—the stretch of ankle the razor misses. "I have never had so much foreplay in my whole life!"

A whole night of it, in fact. They never even bothered with the "play." "He was clearly a sensitive guy, in every sense of the word. He was kind of vulnerable, and there was an emotional quotient there that you don't usually get with someone you've just met. He never even tried to have sex, and I didn't want to force it."

Then, the next day, one of the thousand kisses turns into a dark-red splotch on her neck. She doesn't remember him giving her a hickey, but there it is. She's flying to L.A., where she will see Stefan and her West Coast bosses. She spends her last two hours at the hotel pool trying to sunburn her neck, and she thinks about canceling her flight and spending another night with Leo.

"It just seems as if I've been in a series of relationships my entire adult life, and they are adding up to a long list of obligations: fly, drive, sit, get carsick in a taxi, get dressed, make small talk, be nice. I just wanted to drive around Atlanta with my freelance video director."

And there is the problem of her neck.

She calls Leo from her hotel before she leaves and tells him that she is leaving for L.A. to meet a man that she has been seeing. But she wants him to know she's having second thoughts. He made her realize what she's been missing (approximately 999 kisses). He shows up at the airport to say good-bye, and just before she boards her flight, she leans in and sucks on his neck.

*   *   *

STEFAN IS NERVOUS. He is pacing around their hotel room, fidgeting with his tie. "You're not going to wear *that?*" he says when Casey pulls a red dress out of a garment bag. Apparently not. Stefan is a control freak. He is used to issuing directives. Casey used to hear people around the office joking about him. She liked to think that she brought out the best in him, but now he is being himself, the one she was warned about. He didn't even think to ask about her trip to Atlanta.

She comes out of the shower with her hair up in a towel and starts pulling more clothes out of her bag. She holds up a black dress. He looks over at it for several seconds, then nods. She will be wearing black tonight. "You're going to wear stockings, aren't you?" he says as she disappears into the bathroom. It's July, in Los Angeles, and she just came from a heavy-metal concert shoot. She slides on a pair of itchy sheer nylons.

When she sees her reflection in the bathroom mirror, Casey lets out a gasp. The red blotch has spread and turned purple. Had he seen it? Would he have said something if he had? Maybe he is waiting until later. She dries her hair into a shag, pulling the ends forward to drape her neck. Then she smears too-pale foundation on the splotch and accidentally gets some on her dress. "Hurry up!" he yells. She tries to wipe her dress with a wet washcloth, but her hand shakes and the makeup turns into a beige smudge.

Dinner, at a twenty-room Tudor mansion in Beverly Hills, features an entire staff of people to wait on the guests. Casey spots one of her L.A. bosses and tells him all about her trip to Atlanta. Then she spends twenty minutes talking to another boss about the European record market. When she finally looks around to find Stefan, he is staring at her from across the living room, his eyes are glassy, and she feels a tug somewhere. "I'm mad at myself for being mad at this guy who has treated me to so much. I'm having a great time."

But in the middle of dinner, she starts thinking about Atlanta, about how she just wants to drive around Atlanta with Leo.

Back in New York, she calls to report in with the story about her splotch. "He probably didn't know what it was. I don't think they give hickeys in Holland."

THE END OF July is crazy with obligations. All the bands are on their summer concert tours, and Casey does not have a night off for two weeks. This is convenient; she is again trying to avoid Stefan. They ended up sleeping together in L.A., and it felt like a big mistake.

Leo calls from Atlanta on her second night back. "How's Stefan?" he asks in the first half-minute. She tells him that things are bad between them. "So why don't you stop seeing him?" he asks in a taut voice. Casey sighs. Things have been bad with Stefan for a very long time.

"It's not that simple," she says finally. "I have over ten years invested in this. He's my mentor and one of my closest friends." What she can't tell Leo about is what she tells her friends about: the sushi dinners and the career coaching, the excitement and the security. That when she is with Stefan, she doesn't have to worry about the next life phase. He *is* the next life phase.

Leo is leaving to work a fight in Las Vegas, and he asks Casey to meet him there. She daydreams about this for a day before her boss makes it clear she cannot get away. Instead, she books a flight to Atlanta for the following weekend. "I still think people come into your life for a reason," she says. "Before our big weekend, Leo had been waiting around for some girl in Atlanta to come back. But then he realized how screwed up the whole thing was."

Meanwhile, Stefan has apologized again. He wanted her to know how great it was to have her with him in L.A., how great she looked. He has made a reservation at Tsunami for Thursday night, and he'd like her to come.

"WE'VE GOT TO have a shag before we go out," Stefan says to Casey. He's arrived early at her apartment to pick her up for their sushi date. He's high from drinks with a music agent and he's practically leering at her. She looks over at him, blinks, and tells him she needs to take a shower.

"I am in the shower, thinking—Just get this over with so you can go home and pack for Atlanta. I can't believe it's come to this." In the shower, she starts thinking about Leo again. He told her yesterday that she'd pulled him out of his cocoon. With Stefan, she's a vamp out of a lingerie catalog. With Leo, she's a healer!

There's another problem. Leo hit a nerve. He told Casey she is too much a product of what she does for work. She needs to be more of a kid, get back to her kid self, he told her. She has never met anyone in her world so free from the tunnel grind of work. And he is right. She has lost sight of herself, lost sight of where work ends and *people* begin. (He is "people," Stefan is "work," he seemed to be telling her.)

Forty-five minutes later, when Casey emerges, shriveled, from her shower, Stefan is lying on her bed tapping the remote. He hasn't even thought to ask her why she is going to Atlanta. He reaches forward and tries to pull off her towel. She is shaking. Having sex with this man has become an item on her to-do list. She starts a fight with him about his drinking and kicks him out.

Jen

WHILE CASEY WAS flying to L.A. to meet Stefan, Jen was flying to New York. She didn't want to spend her favorite holiday in the hot smog. When she was little, she wore an Uncle Sam hat and red seersucker shorts in the Newton Fourth of July parade. Everyone would come out and cheer. Jen had to get out of town, and since Becca and Alex are in Vegas for the weekend, Nate is hosting his new girlfriend, and even her parents are away, she has no choice but to go to New York.

Only Fiona knows she's coming. The truth is, Jen isn't that excited about heading back to New York so soon after she sewed the whole place up in her head. She doesn't want to be let down again, and one way to ensure this is to strip away all expectations. But some friends of Fiona's are throwing a thirtieth birthday party on an old rusty lightship. Jen's own thirtieth is only a week away. But she's decided not to tell anyone. (If no one knows, it never happened.) And, by setting up meetings on Thursday, she can get work to pay for it, so she stays in a nice hotel. She catches the red-eye on Wednesday night and checks into the St. Regis Thursday morning.

The party, Friday night, takes place on an abandoned pier on the Hudson where the boat is docked. Fiona promises to meet her there at nine. Jen shows up alone, nervous and playing with the straps on her new sari print dress. She looks around and notices the abundance of striking men gathered around an outdoor bar. She does not recognize any of them, and they are not even trying to recognize her. She remembers Fiona telling her that the birthday girl works for a shoe designer.

"Breeders to the left," a tall woman is gurgling through her drink. "I'm not navigating my way through all those tanned-and-tender cheekbones," she says to Jen. "They've got to self-sort before I make my way."

Jen recognizes the woman as Francie, a friend of Fiona's from work. The two of them head to the bar together. They can't find anyone they know, and they can't find any men who want to talk to them.

They order vodka tonics and Jen scours the boat for Fiona. She finally spots her up on deck talking to, of all people, Max. Ugh. She takes a deep breath. Max still hasn't told Jen he's getting married. A few months ago, he called her from a friend's office, explaining that Sara doesn't like his talking to her. He neglected to mention that Sara was now his fiancée.

Jen finishes her vodka and heads up on deck to say hi. "I've got some really big news to tell you," Max whispers into her ear when he sees her.

"What could that be?" she says, pushing up her cheeks.

"I broke the band up this week."

That would be his big news? Jen pretends to listen to him tell the story of his band's divorce. Pretty soon he'll run out of material and realize he has nowhere else to turn. But the next thing she knows, they are engulfed by Max's tribe of college friends, dark-haired boys in vintage shirts. Justin the filmmaker is there, but he is surrounded by his friends, not making eye contact. Jen grabs another vodka tonic and heads inside the boat. She wanders around the dark rusty levels for what seems like an hour, lost and alone with her drink. This is her Fourth of July? Wandering around a dirty old boat full of gay men and lounge boys in her estranged city? Where the hell is everyone? She is trying to make out a face peering over a railing when a blond, boyish man approaches her. He grabs her drink, heads to the corner, and deposits it. Then he walks back to her, grabs both of her hands, and pulls her to a dark dance floor. She is leaning back, feet gripping her slides, which are gripping the floor. When she looks up, two bright blue eyes are gazing into hers. They are beautiful. She remembers mostly this: he spun her in a circle until her feet came up off the ground; he let go once and she was on the floor; her back made a small sound when he dipped her; and then her hair graced the tarmac.

After what seemed like hours, the man-boy pulls her off the dance floor and leads her down a hallway to the captain's quarters—a half-moon room with a couched banquette, swinging lights, and people. His name is Patrick. He is a baby brother, the last of eight, and just out of college.

Jen's not really listening to him. She can't stop staring at his hair. He has thick, tamed, dirty-blond hair—which surrenders into bottom curls—and yellow-brown sideburns. "I've never been so close to so much beautiful hair in my life," she giggles as she pets his head. He leans in and kisses her, and the room falls silent. Jen pulls away when she realizes who he is.

"Are you Elizabeth's little brother?" she asks nervously. Elizabeth works with Fiona. They all went out once when Jen came to New York, and someone was talking about Elizabeth's little brother.

"I'm the youngest," he says rolling up his eyes. "But I have an old soul. I grew up with older parents and a six pack of older sisters. They taught me how to dance and they forbade me to watch Barbie Benton on *Fantasy Island*."

This was all she needed. Actually, she didn't need anything. He's the Little Prince! The Little Prince, kissing her in the captain's quarters. Downstairs, the DJ is playing "Come on Eileen." Jen decides she is in love.

FIONA GETS A call at ten the next morning from the St. Regis.

"What happened?"

"I clubbed him and dragged him back to the hotel." Jen is giggling.

"Is he still there?"

"He's asleep on the big white rug in the bathroom."

"What?"

"Our room was really hot last night. I think it's cooler in there."

"I can't believe you kidnapped Elizabeth's baby brother. What the hell happened?"

"I don't know. All of a sudden we're all over each other in a cab. I kept stumbling. I just can't wear those platform slides anymore. It's like Big Bird on skates."

"Spill!"

"His hair! I've never seen so much beautiful hair in my whole life."

"You're still drunk."

"He ran off with someone's camera from the party, and I took a picture of his hair. Then he took a picture of the gold slippers by my bed." Jen lets out a loud belly laugh, then cuts herself down to a whisper. "The hotel left two pairs of these gold slippers by the . . ."

"Did you sleep with him?"

"Um, no."

"Did you?" Fiona asks again.

"No! And you're not telling Elizabeth any of this."

"I don't need to. He already called her from your bathroom phone this morning."

"*What?*"

"He slept through work. He called her because he's afraid he lost his job."

"And she called you?"

"She called Francie, who called me."

"Oh, God. I'm so embarrassed." Jen is picturing Elizabeth.

"Why is he still there?"

"I don't know. I woke up and thought he was gone. Then I tried to go to the bathroom. I think I talked him out of going to work early this morning."

"Well, now you're going to have to write him a note and get him a new job." Fiona is only half kidding.

"Not . . . funny."

WHEN PATRICK FINALLY emerges, he is wearing a big white St. Regis bathrobe, bottom curls clinging to terrycloth. He jumps into bed with Jen and starts tickling her. Then he runs to the bathroom and gets them both a glass of water. This innocence goes on, according to Jen, until noon, when the hotel maid kicks them out.

Jen spends the weekend with Fiona at her summer share house on Long Island. Phase two of her hangover isn't pretty. Her head and tailbone hurt from when he dropped her. She keeps flinching every time she thinks about his sister, calling his other sister, calling another sister. Apparently they burned up the phone lines from Seattle to D.C., trying to figure out if Patrick was turning into a character in a Jay McInerney novel.

"That hair," Jen finally says on the Sunday train ride home. She is in recovery.

"Are you ready to confess?" Fiona asks.

"I did confess. Nothing really happened."

"You think I'm going to buy that?"

"He's an angel boy."

"What did you do to the angel boy?"

"In the middle of the night, he reached over and held my hand." Jen grins and looks out the window.

"Oh, please. He could be your son."

"Thank God I never married Evan. He never would have grown cool sideburns like that."

"I'm not listening until you . . ."

"Okay. I told him we couldn't have sex, and then I put on my 'don't touch me' nightgown, the white cotton one with the little straps and the satin bow . . ."

"The one that looks like a training bra?"

"Uh-huh. So of course he was all over this. He was really ticklish, so I kept tickling him. He said, 'If you keep doing this, you're going to end up on the other side of the room.' So, I did it again, and next thing you know, I'm on the floor. I felt like Thelma."

"You vixen."

"I was not a vixen. We refrained . . . somehow." Fiona shoots her a look. "There's just one detail I left out."

"Mm?"

"Well, at one point he jumped up on the bed. I had a flashback: I'm baby-sitting for the Mahoneys, and there is Buddy Mahoney, before the Ritalin, jumping on his parents' bed."

Anna

LIKE JEN, ANNA wants to spend the Fourth of July in New York. Her reasons have less to do with childhood memories than with adult pangs. "I can't get laid in this city," she says one day in late June. "I'm going to New York."

Actually, her friends from college are getting married on Saturday just outside the city, and when she found out that her ex-husband wasn't going, she booked an expensive last-minute flight.

She spends Thursday night in Manhattan with her friend Henry. He was her account executive for six months when she worked in New York, and he quickly became her volunteer counseling corps. She was in the middle of separating from Greg, and he teased her through the torture.

"He's gay and very 'over it,'" she explains. "He laughs at everything. And he just gets it, the pain part. You don't have to say anything. The look on your face just tells him. And then he's making fun of you and you're over it too."

They meet Henry's friend John at the Universal Grill in the West Village, and before dinner comes, the boys both start in on her.

"How's Mr. Denim-on-Denim?" John asks Anna.

"I told John about the Bad Cowboy," Henry explains to Anna. "He came up with a new title for him."

"I think you should pick him up some denim socks and a nice denim Gap cap," John says.

"A nice denim Baby Gap hat," Anna says nodding.

"Oh, Henry told me about that. Bad cowbabies. I didn't know they made denim-on-denim diapers. We should invest in those, Henry."

"We should. How about denim wipes?" Henry watches Anna carefully. "Anna, that man's baggage is getting too big to fit in the overhead. I don't think you should let him do any more boarding."

She spends Friday the Fourth in Central Park with her friend Michelle. They shared an apartment in college, and they are both going to the wedding tomorrow. Anna and Michelle used to spend a lot of time together when they both lived in D.C. in their early twenties. Michelle lived with three women in a railroad flat in Arlington; Anna and Greg shared a beautiful apartment in Georgetown. Michelle characterizes this as her dark phase: two unpaid jobs, a string of dates with a certified misogynist and a Redskins bookie. She would ride her bike to Anna and Greg's to escape her roommates, and her growing cynicism about D.C.'s twenty-five-or-bust marriage domino effect.

Seven years, a marriage, a divorce, and two cities later, Anna and Michelle are now sitting in Central Park's Boat House Café, looking out at the rowboats and the ducks. Michelle wants to talk to Anna about San Francisco. She has just fallen in love, and she is thinking of pulling up stakes and heading west to be with him.

"Last time I saw you, you were lonely and bored. Now I'm lonely and bored," Anna tells Michelle.

"Oh, God, I don't want to relive D.C."

"But you had fun with Greg and me when you were lonely, didn't you?"

"I did. I loved my Anna and Greg time. You two were like Lucy and Desi. You were a show we all bought tickets for."

"I know, we were like cluster birds," Anna says, as if confessing something.

"I used to whine to you that I was never going to meet my soulmate."

"And I would say, You will! Look at me, I met Greg! There are more Gregs out there . . . ready to turn into your brother. You, at least, had a sex life."

"If that's what you want to call it." Michelle's face contorts as she flips through the images.

"You always seemed to be having fun," Anna says, remembering her envy.

"Are you kidding? You were married, you were a couple, so I didn't really confide in you then."

"Yeah. As much as my married friends try to listen to me now, there's a barrier there," Anna admits.

"Well, you don't want to bring them down."

"No, I'll bring them down. They're just not joining me in my trash session. And this is no fun."

"We bonded over work and college," Michelle says. "We didn't really get into the trashing boys stuff. When you first left Greg, I was so mad at you. I remember thinking—how can she leave the greatest guy, the greatest relationship, when the rest of us have nothing?"

"I know, everyone was, like, 'If she thinks she can find someone better, she's wrong!' "

"Well, when we said you two were like brother and sister, we didn't know you were really . . . like brother and sister. It just sounded cute." Michelle shrugs.

"It's cute until you remember that you never had sex with your brother, and that you are never going to have a real sex life again."

"Do you think that happens to everyone eventually?"

"No. But I think it happens to people who marry for security, emotional or financial or whatever. I think it gets better in the right relationship. Love changes and evolves. You get sick of each other, but there is something in the middle of it all that sticks."

Their friends Gary and Allison have stuck. They've been together since they were twenty-two; and now that they're ready to have kids, they've finally decided to get married. They're holding their wedding on the lawn of an old Georgian manor overlooking the Hudson River, and they've invited all their college friends. They're in their early thirties now, which means that a few of their friends are already divorced. The same effect that triggers the early marriages seems to trigger the early splits.

Anticipating a little awkwardness, the bride and groom hold a "mobile" reception, an hors d'oeuvres cocktail hour followed by a buffet with self-selected seating. The idea is that the single people won't be so keenly aware that they are dateless, and no one gets cornered talking to the same strange table mates for two hours.

This is just what Anna needs. She and Michelle take the train up together on Saturday. They both circle the reception, catching up with everyone. Anna runs into people from each phase of her adult life, from each of her frontiers: sophomore year, senior year, D.C., Chicago, New York. "I suddenly remembered that I had all these other friends, really great, wonderful friends," she says later. "I'm not out there all by myself. And none of these people even know about the bad cowboy."

One of Anna's old roommates brought her baby, a giggling one-year-old, and all the adults took turns giggling with her. "My roommate was so happy it was infectious, just so sincere and real. It gave me hope. I can imagine it when I see her. She has the greatest husband and they're in love with each other. The world is full of bad examples, and they're a shining example."

Anna has always wanted kids. She wanted to get pregnant during her first year of marriage, when she was twenty-five, but Greg thought they should wait until they had more money. "I need to have kids, I know that. They just crack me up. But I have no interest in being a single parent, because then I would be an abusive parent."

She admits that she is not exactly drawn to the dad species. The last person who came close was Greg. He would have been the perfect dad. "He was caring and generous and warmhearted, completely nonjudgmental and fair. And he would never run with scissors."

Then again, her brother would make a good dad too, but she doesn't want to have kids with him.

"Do you have to sacrifice romance and passion and sex to have kids?" she asks pleadingly. "How many people would take that bargain . . . I mean, if they knew that going into it?"

Anna is turning thirty-two soon, but she is relatively calm about the time pressure to have kids. "I still think of myself as young. I've got time."

There has been soothing news for baby panickers. In May, a sixty-five-year-old woman gave birth to a healthy baby, breaking the age record. Then a fifty-one-year-old woman in Georgia gave birth to healthy twins from eggs that she had frozen more than a decade earlier. Next came a PBS report revealing that the idea of waning fertility after age thirty-five might be a myth—the same women who have problems before thirty-five have problems later. It's not clear how much age really matters anymore.

Biological stakes aside, Anna has become a believer in older parenthood. "Some of the greatest people I know had older parents—moms who gave birth in their forties—and they have great relationships with their parents. I don't buy into this fear of older parents. The best parents are the unselfish kind, and I'm going to be pretty damn sick of myself by the time I'm forty."

Then she stops for a minute and starts counting. "Yikes. I am going to be thirty-five in three years. You can't be thirty-five and single in San Francisco! Everybody wants to know why. If I'm not in a serious relationship by the time I'm thirty-five, I'm definitely moving to New York. People try to set you up all the time in New York. There are tons of great guys who are single and divorced there who are ready to have kids." She pauses to imagine them for a minute. "And I will be there to service them."

Jen

It's a Tuesday, and Jen is back in L.A. She is afraid to call her sister. New York is getting big again. Big with a baby brother. Becca will not be excited about her story. Becca will tell her she is a *manizer*. She will tell her New York brings out the worst in her, that she is regressing.

Even her cats are mad at her. They sensed betrayal the minute she unlocked the front door. Rudy keeps flattening his ears and twitching his head away when she calls him. She reaches down to scratch his neck, and he sprints away. She remembers what Becca said before she left — she thinks Rudy might be gay. This momentarily frees Jen from her guilt.

It's ten o'clock at night, and Jen won't be able to sleep until she talks this thing back into proportion. She decides to call Fiona. "What if he's ruined me for all others?"

"It's one in the morning here."

"I'm sorry. Are you sleeping? I just wanted to see how the rest of your weekend went," Jen lies.

"No, I haven't talked to Elizabeth yet."

"That's not why I was calling."

"We went to a movie. Then I told Dan I needed sleep." Fiona emphasizes the word "sleep."

"Fiona, how can I face all of these . . ."

"Men?"

"Yeah. Men. I need fresh-faced innocence. I need an angel boy."

Rudy jumps up onto Jen's bed and starts kneading her stomach. "Your angel boy is a devilish man in training," Fiona says, yawning. "Besides, he lives three thousand miles away. He is twenty-three years old. And you knew him for approximately four drunken hours."

"Twelve. The problem is, I have standards now. Life was moving along fine without standards. I walked by these *GQ* models in the airport today, and I looked them in the eye and thought—you're just not him."

Rudy's ear twitches. Fiona is right. Later, Jen decides that she needs to put Patrick in a little box, "with a bow on it," and preserve the night. In the meantime, she's decided that standards are not such a bad thing. They elevate the gaze, she decides, keep you from getting mired in bad relationships. Keep you from . . . reality.

THE FOLLOWING WEEK, she spends her days at work E-mailing people in New York. She's managed to turn thirty without much fanfare—just a low-key dinner with her sister—and is focusing on her future instead. Evan, her ex, mentioned a job at a film company in TriBeCa last month, so she sends him a note asking about it. It's always good to keep your options open, she tells herself. She could be out of a job someday. Becca would kill her.

Nate calls on Thursday. "Where have you been?" he says when she pushes the button to her private line. She completely forgot about Nate, and this time she wasn't even trying to forget. Nate is always pining over some girl in New York. He will be sympathetic to her withdrawal symptoms. She meets him for a drink and tells him about her weekend.

"I thought the reason we couldn't date was that I was too young?" he says after a long silence. Nate is two years Jen's junior, and they couldn't date because he wouldn't stop talking about some faraway woman. But this just figures. Nate's a lot like Rudy. He waits until Jen is distracted and starts pushing his paws back into her. He apparently had a bad weekend with his rock goddess—that's what happens when you take them out of the box.

He tells Jen that he's been thinking they should move in together. "Can you imagine the place we'd have? We'd both be rich!"

Jen lets out a half-laugh and slurps her drink. Then she looks up and stares at his hair—limp brown and straight as reeds. "We're in love, aren't we?" he says.

"You are really starting to remind me of my cat," she says, blowing bubbles through her straw.

She gets home in time for *Seinfeld* and a phone call from Evan in New York. He is upset. He is in the process of losing his girlfriend, and he's thinking of coming to L.A..

"What happened?" Jen asks with genuine concern.

"I refused to go on vacation with her."

"Oh. Did you tell her you wouldn't even go to Connecticut with me?"

"No. It's not . . . It's just that . . . There are all these NYU students in my neighborhood and I keep looking at them and having dirty thoughts."

Jen sighs into the phone and turns up the volume on her remote.

"You're a dirty old man, Evan," she says.

"Jen." Evan is chuckling into her ear.

"What?"

"You're a dirty old woman." Jen groans, then gets quiet. What a horrible thought. "You see, now you understand," he says.

"I am. I'm a dirty old woman."

"It all goes back to puberty," Evan says. "It sucked going through it, but nothing will ever compare. We just want to feel the way we did when we hit puberty."

"Ashamed and smelly?"

"No. Excited and . . . scared."

"I never understood how smart, successful men could date twenty-year-old women," Jen says. "What do they talk about? And after a while, don't they feel like they're with a blow-up doll? What intrigue could these women possibly hold for them?"

"So . . . what is the intrigue of the young, clueless, career-less man?"

"He reminds you of a more excitable life phase?"

"Yeah. Or your libido stood still. Locked in seventh-grade health class."

This is why Jen and Evan couldn't last. They deconstructed their libidos together. They deconstructed *everything* together. There was really no hope of constructing romance out of the rubble. And this is why she needs a young, fresh-faced boy. Patrick is still a builder! He hasn't turned into a giant wrecking ball.

* * *

THE NEXT DAY, Jen gets a call from Justin the filmmaker. She forgot that she sent him an E-mail. He asks her if she can set him up with a few meetings the next time he comes to L.A. She pictures him staring into his drink at the Hollywood Spin. If anyone needs her help, it is Justin. She is writing down names on a Post-it when her assistant yells in: "Somebody named Patrick on line one."

Jen freezes. No last name. It must be him. It hits her for a minute that he is younger than her assistant. She clears her throat and presses the lit button. "Hello?"

"This is the St. Regis Hotel in New York. A pair of golden slippers were taken from room 1014 last Thursday and we have reason to believe you have them."

"Oh, no," Jen laughs nervously into the phone. *Oh, no,* she has to come up with something to say. When she was in college, a Seven Sisters school in New England, she and her friends took road trips to the coed schools and attempted to do all the things they thought other people did in college. Then they drove back to their little campus and hid. This time, she's been found.

"Did you lose your job?" she asks after a long pause.

"Not yet. But I hope you're lining up a movie deal for me out there. My internship ends next month."

"I've felt horrible about keeping you from an internship? They never fire interns."

"They came very close to firing this intern last month."

"Oh, I'm really sorry."

"No. It was worth it."

She is about to ask him if he has any trips planned to L.A. when her boss comes into her office, yelling. "I've got to go," she says quickly and hangs up.

Jen spends her lunch break at her desk, doodling on her Post-its, biting the insides of her cheeks. "James on line one," her assistant yells in, breaking her daze. Ugh. The ponytailed writer. Little does he know how badly he will suffer—rumpled blond locks and all—for his timing. She wasn't that crazy about him before she developed standards. Now a jumbo jug of ginseng caplets couldn't give this guy chemistry. They talk about his latest screenplay, then he invites her to see Radiohead, her favorite band. Becca did tell her to give him a second chance. Not even a full minute after she takes him up on his offer, he asks her if she can put him in touch with a big agent. "Oh," she says, clicking back in. Networking day at Jen Enterprises. "I'll look into it."

Quid pro quo. She starts to wonder if this is why he asked her out to begin with. She thought he already had an agent. She has been talking herself into liking this guy! Even innocent Patrick thinks she can make him into a movie star. Justin, Patrick, ponytail . . . She starts braiding them together in her head when her assistant comes in with a chef salad. Jen barely touches it.

She calls to see if Emily is free for coffee. Emily has been in L.A. a lot longer and knows all about being hustled. It's bad enough that they had to spend their adolescence wondering if the guys just wanted to get into their pants. Now they have to worry that the guys are just trying to get into their Rolodexes.

They go to the Coffee Bean and Tea Leaf in Venice and order sugar-free Iced Blendeds. Emily was a drama major in college, which makes her a certified dating consultant. Jen's trouble, Emily says, is that she gives off platonic vibes. "I've seen you with Nate. You treat him like a brother." This is true, Jen realizes for a moment. She remembers blowing bubbles into her drink while he watched.

"I hardly treated Patrick like a brother," she says.

"Well, you have to separate Patrick from the rest. He is not a Hollywood hustler. Yet."

"They all start to blur together after a while."

"Next time you are with Nate, don't talk about your other relationships. And don't look past him every two seconds to see who else is going to walk through the door.

"But he's doing that to me!"

"Well, it's up to you to break the cycle. For all you know he's doing that because you are. And try to touch his arm a few times."

"Oh, Emily. Don't tell me you're one of them."

"What?"

"Eew. I've seen the starlets do that. It's so phony-baloney."

"It's about showing interest."

"I'll work on my eye contact," Jen says.

Anna

BACK AT HER desk after her trip to New York, Anna is reading a Frommer's guide to Greece. New York cured her loneliness bug, and now she has to work on her adventure bug. "People get laid in Greece," she explains. She is determined to forget the bad cowboy, and one way she thinks she will be able to do this is by finding someone even worse. A bad European playboy.

Ethan has been leaving her messages, but she hasn't bothered to return them. The last time they spoke, he told her he was having "fan-ta-sies" about her. "I'm supposed to be the benchwarmer here, waiting for my big shot on the field. Fantasy girl sleeps alone, reality girl gets the man every night." She pauses to mull that over for a few seconds, then adds, "I've been reality girl. She sleeps alone, too. When the bad cowboys are involved, the bottom line is that no one has anyone."

Besides, she's not sure what they would have to talk about now. Lamaze classes? She has desensitized herself, her therapist told her. Your feelings can be hurt only so much before they simply go away.

"I think I got over everything on the July Fourth weekend," she says calling in from work one day. "I saw so many old friends that I didn't miss Greg anymore. There was much more to my past than Greg. And I've pretty much run the gamut of emotions on Ethan: bitter, angry, free. Ethan was just about getting through the divorce."

She's over Greg. She's over the anti-Greg, Ethan. Now she's trying to imagine something in the middle, but she can't. Getting over people doesn't always solve your problems. "For the first time

I've just realized how hard this is — being single. Until now, I never really focused on it. There was Greg, the divorce, Ethan, leftover Greg. There was moving twice in three years. New jobs." Now the drama is over, and she's left with the great plain that is her life.

She decides to call her unemployed friend Ben to see if he still wants to write a screenplay with her. Ben was a year behind Anna in college, and they ran into each other when Anna first moved to San Francisco. They went out drinking late one night after a college reunion, and they hashed out a screenplay idea: This man and this woman are the last two remaining single people from a group of college friends. They get these wedding invitations that say "And Guest" and they have two weeks to find dates. "She tries to get a brass ring guy. He goes through the personality parade," Anna explains. "What initially attracts them becomes repulsive: the sexy guy becomes a greasy slut; the perfect wife is a bore."

They haven't figured out the ending yet. But Anna has written her Oscar speech. "I stand up and I thank every man I've loved — I'm all boobs and legs — thank them for empowering me to be this angry." Ben points out that most of those men won't be watching the Academy Awards. They talk about writing a Superbowl ad instead.

Then the phone rings, and Anna picks it up without thinking. "Oh, hi," she says, making a face at Ben. It's Ethan. She was just starting to have some fun with her make-believe drama. She really doesn't need this reality in her face. He tells her he's going to Italy for a few months because Sophia wants to have the baby there. He says he just wanted her to know that he's going to be out of the country for a while.

"That's . . . good to know," she tells him. She has opened a bag of Fritos and is chomping into the phone. He starts telling her he's nervous about seeing Sophia, the mother of his child. He hasn't seen her in a while, and they're going to have to do the "getting to know you" again thing.

When she brings this up later, she can't hide her anger. He seems to know how to get to her, how to give his "legacy" in her life emotional heft. He lets her in on a confidence that betrays the other woman. He *knows* Anna, he seems to be telling her; he doesn't know Sophia.

"Okay," Anna says to Ben after she hangs up, "he's having a baby with this woman and he has to get to know her again? While she's pregnant?"

"Is this Mr. Best-Sex-in-the-World?" Ben asks.

"No. He is Mr. Best-Sex-Until-I-Get-Laid-in-Greece. The thing is—good sex is so important to him, I know he's freaking out because she's probably not into it anymore. So he has to call me or some other woman. In the layer cake that is his life, it goes: Ethan, Ethan's baby, Ethan, Sophia, Ethan, Anna, Ethan, Ethan . . . with Ethan frosting."

Ben and Anna give up on their screenplay for the night.

August

I (and most men) don't like pressuring a woman to make a commitment. At some level, we feel like we shouldn't have to pressure her. Aren't women (men think) supposed to crave lifelong connection? And aren't *we* the prize?

—Jackson Park,

quoted in *Elle* magazine

Casey

IT'S AUGUST. The stock market is teetering, a woman in North Carolina just successfully sued her husband's lover for wrecking her marriage, the Supreme Court has ruled that Paula Jones can sue a sitting president for a seven-year-old sexual harassment incident, and it's Elvis Week in Memphis.

These are strange times, Casey thinks, teetering just a little at her desk. Leo, her Atlanta man, hasn't called in over a week. She was talking to him every other day, then every other other day, then not even once a week. Their plans to see each other again fell through, and he was never very good over the phone. And then she got busy with work. Her boss was happy with the Atlanta shoot and scheduled her to do two more in Boston and Philadelphia — on top of her daily workload. Now she is swamped with phone calls and videotapes and schedules and travel arrangements.

One of the calls she needs to return is her mother's. Her younger cousin is getting married this weekend in Baltimore, and her parents want to make sure she will be there. She calls her brother and asks him to help her get out of it.

"I am just so crazed with work, Brett."

"You know Mom and Dad want to see you," he says tersely. "And they want you to be happy. They really don't care if you *ever* get married."

Ugh. Where did that come from? This must be the family conversation they have when she's not around. Casey starts to wonder — do her parents worry about what the relatives think? Do they wonder where they went wrong with her? Her twenty-five-year-old cousins will be there with spouses.

She wears her red sleeveless dress to the wedding and arrives late with a plastic grin. "You look *won*-der-ful!" her aunt says, holding out her arms when she sees her. Her father winks at her from over her aunt's shoulder.

"Look at my niece!" her uncle says, hugging her. "What's wrong with those men in New York? Why isn't my beautiful niece walking down that aisle?"

"Oh, I'm having too much fun, Uncle Roger," she says, tilting her head.

Her four-year-old nephew Timothy lets out a shriek when he first sees her. He runs over and grabs her fingers and pulls her around the reception hall. He stops to pull a berry off a plate and tries to throw it into her mouth. She will never have a better wedding date. She takes him to the dance floor and holds his hand as he spins in circles.

Casey is squatting down to do the bump with Timothy when a man approaches her and asks if he can cut in. He looks like Major Nelson. Young Larry Hagman, back when he owned Genie. He's loaded on mai tais, and he's wearing suede shoes and an unbuttoned shirt, showing off his hairy chest. Casey tries to keep Timothy dancing between them, but he gets jealous and runs to his mom. The man grabs Casey's hand, puts it on his shoulder, and pulls her close. Behind him she can see Timothy burying his head in his mother's neck.

At the end of the night, Major Nelson asks Casey for her phone number, and she writes it on a wedding napkin. On her way out, her uncle gives her a hug good-bye and some teary end-of-wedding advice. "Don't you rush into anything, Casey. You have your fun, hon."

Major Nelson calls Casey the following week and invites her to an early screening of *Boogie Nights*. His friend knows one of the producers. He picks her up at her apartment with his shirt only loosely buttoned, chest hair sticking out of the top. "But I'm actually thinking he's sexy. The movie is just two hours of casual sex and I suddenly just really need to have sex. And, boy, did this guy ask for it. I mean if you are going to wear your shirt like that, you are going to hook up with me."

Casey is dizzy with a newfound freedom. She feels free from Stefan, free from Leo. She is no longer obligated to be a vamp or a healer. She is no longer obligated to feel bad, let down. She is no longer obligated to feel anything.

Back in her apartment the following day, Casey is giggling to herself about her night with hairy Larry Hagman when she gets a call from Andrew, a reporter she met at a work party last spring. She flips by his card every couple of days in her Rolodex and wonders about him. They had talked about going to a Yankees game. When she calls him back, he invites her to see a Natalie Merchant concert next month. "That sounds great," she says, beaming. From Markey Mark to Natalie Merchant. Sometimes her life is a little tough to reconcile.

And then it gets even better. Her friend Margot calls two days later from Chicago to tell her that her brother Dave is in New York mixing a commercial soundtrack. She thinks they should get together. Casey has met Dave several times over the years. He is tall and dark-skinned with a European face and a midwestern build, and she started shaking once when she had to sit next to him at a family dinner. He was always seeing someone, or she was seeing someone. Now they're both alone. "I'm on a tear," she recalls one night. "Doing really well at work. Fixing up my apartment. Ready to go. I could get Bill Clinton on the phone. So . . . I call him."

DAVE RETURNS HER call, and the Friday before Labor Day weekend finds Casey sitting next to him in a recording studio. He had to work all week, odd evening hours, so he invited her to come and watch him. In the dark padded room, she tries to make out his face in the blue light of the studio. He has big, veined forearms, and she keeps sneaking looks at them. Then she sneaks looks at the rest of him. "I was thinking, 'Someone keeps holding a big candy bar in front of me, saying, go on, one more bite. I'm addicted to the sugar rush.'"

After he finishes the recording, they leave the studio and walk down Broadway with no real plan. She talks about live concert shoots, Elvis, how she would have loved to work on his albums. He talks about electronic sound mixing. When she tells him she should probably hail a cab, he insists on giving her a ride home. No one in New York has ever insisted on giving her a ride anywhere. His car is parked in a garage a few blocks away. On the way to her apartment, Casey looks over at him and tries to imagine them dating. The vision just doesn't come to her. "I couldn't feel a thing. It's very scary when you are with your perfect type and you cannot feel a thing."

When she gets home, she calls Stefan and asks him if he wants to see a band with her this weekend. She always felt something with Stefan, even if it was occasionally disgust. She hasn't been out with someone she feels comfortable with for a long time. "I don't think so, Casey," he says briskly. "I have company."

Casey tosses the phone onto her couch, falls onto her bed, and starts to cry. Then she starts to sob, wheezing breaths of dead air and stuttering sniffles. It's Labor Day weekend and she is all by herself, stuck in the city. Even Stefan is no longer there for her. Her whole body shakes until she finally falls asleep, still dressed in her jeans and underwire bra.

She wakes up Saturday morning and starts spackling her bathroom. There are holes and cracks everywhere that haven't been filled since she moved in. She is lost in spatula work when Dave calls and invites her to his parents' summer house out on Long Island. It sounds like some sort of family gathering. Casey carries the phone into the bathroom. She has a smear of white Spackle on her face and dark smudges under her eyes. She tells him no. After a long sigh, she tells him that she'll think about it and call him in the morning.

She sets a goal to paint until *Saturday Night Live,* and at 11:30, still finishing the bathroom trim, she pushes the remote with her big toe. There is a news break, which looks like the opening of the show, but the news is that Princess Diana is dead and the anchor looks pretty real and there doesn't seem to be any punch line. Why would they start a comedy show with this? Casey finally stops painting. She has never paid much attention to the Lady Di saga, but

0

this is horrible. She sees this woman's face more often than her sister's.

She takes a train to Dave's parents' house the next morning. Thirty-six is not that far off, she thinks, staring at the newspapers. And she hasn't even had her prince phase yet. She arrives and realizes that it is just the two of them. His parents are away visiting Margot. Dave looks brown and shiny in a faded college crew shirt. She smiles at him and starts to thaw a little, then gets nervous. Margot told her that he thinks she's a little wild—all the stories about their nights on the town. He's already seen her report card, discussed her. She doesn't like this. On the deck of his parents' house, he tells her that he's glad she came; she smiles coyly down at her crossed arms.

She spends the day learning how to sail. Dave is patient and calm—encouraging her, explaining each line. He is a new coach to teach her new things. He sits her down next to him, holds her hand over the tiller, and shows her how to steer. Then he watches her as she takes the curved wooden handle on her own, beaming at his new pupil. "Push left to turn right," he tells her. She stares up at him for a minute and the boat careens to the left. He jumps up and takes over. "I'm sorry," Casey says, ducking under the sail. "What did I do?" "Nothing," he says laughing. "You did fine. That's just the wind letting you know who's in charge here."

On the walk back to the house, they talk about music. He played wind instruments in grade school, and he has always been into music. "This guy is the real deal. He doesn't care about the record business. It doesn't even come up. And he's not one of my band boys. He's an adult. He's a genuine, strong, sexy man. I'm completely intimidated."

That night they order-in Italian food and rent a Quentin Tarantino movie. He makes a pillow couch for them on the floor, and they sit next to each other, shoulders barely touching. Casey's back starts to cramp, but she is afraid to get comfortable. "I'm trying to figure out how we're going to do this. Where the hell am I going to sleep? And how is this not going to be awkward?" When the movie finally ends, they both start stretching. Casey gets up and walks around, checking out the room situation. "I made up a bed for you in there," he yells from the living room. When she is finished brushing her teeth, he gives her a hug and a quick kiss, then he tells her that he's been wanting to kiss her all day. She climbs into her twin bed and puts her hands over her face. She has never been sent to bed on a date before. The man was tormented all day by the urge to give her a spin-the-bottle kiss?

They spend Labor Day trying to play tennis. Casey knocks balls over the fence and into the net. She is a little frustrated, and tennis is not her sport. She wonders why he had to pick the two things she cannot do. Despite this, Dave rounds up all her lost balls, then tells her she's a natural.

She takes the train back that night. When she wakes up the following morning in her own bed, her face is pink with fever and sunburn. He calls her at work the next day and asks for her E-mail address. He is going to Memphis for two months to mix an album. Casey is relieved. "I'm thinking, this is going to be great—I can get my affairs in order, you know, literally. Bring things to a close."

Jen

"CAN YOU GET us into Sky Bar?"

Two voices are chuckling into Jen's headset. At this point, it could be anyone: the two young actors she met at the *L.A. Confidential* premiere, the ponytailed screenwriter, her parents. It turns out to be Justin, the tortured filmmaker, and Paul, his self-appointed sales rep. Paul is another one of Max's young turk fraternity friends, the brooding short handsome one. Max once wrote a song about Paul's penis: "It's bigger than me . . ." That was the refrain.

Jen tells them she wants to go to dinner first, and they're treating. "If they're going to work me over, they're going to pay for it—like any business-client relationship."

Paul is more striking than she remembers. He has long black

bangs that hang down to his eyes and lines that split his cheek-bones. And Justin is cuter than she remembers. His eyes are a wise blue, lined with long, curly black lashes. He is wearing a fedora and a dark suit; he just came from a meeting. He seems a little more relaxed than usual. He manages to smile at her twice.

Over drinks at the Hollywood Spin, Jen wastes no time prying information out of them.

"So when is Max getting married?" she asks casually.

"I don't know. October?" Paul says, looking over at Justin. Justin shrugs.

"Where are they having it?"

"At Kenny's Castaways on Bleecker Street," Paul says, laughing to Justin. "Max is gonna sing his vows."

"And charge admission," Justin adds.

"Is he still milking everyone?" Jen asks.

"And their mother. Last time I saw him he borrowed two dollars from me to get a hot dog. Then we get to the hot dog stand and he tells me he's not hungry anymore. Never gave me my two dollars back."

"It's good to know he hasn't changed."

"Hey, I almost forgot," Paul says to Jen. "He's one of your exes."

Ha. If only she would almost forget.

When the check comes, Jen looks away. Justin heads for the bathroom. After a few minutes, Paul drops his head, stretches his arm out grudgingly, and reaches for it. Then he starts telling Jen about Justin's latest script. "It's going to be big," he says.

"Since when did you become so savvy about the industry, Paul?"

"Since I told Justin I'm getting a cut."

"Oh, he's paying you to hang out with him?"

"Fuck, yeah. Who do you think told him to wear that hat?"

"You're a one-man mafia, Pauly."

"That's right. And I plan to make a lot of money taking care of Justin Grimaldi."

"Well, my mom always told me to find a nice, ambitious man."

"I'm ambitious! My five-year plan is, I'm going to sit on my ass, watch TV, and pretend I work for Justin Grimaldi."

"You are so shameless," Jen says.

"There's a lot of money in shameless," Paul says, beaming.

"You are a shameless Hollywood wife! And you're not even gay."

"Jen, please. I'm a trophy boy. I'm a straight Italian trophy boy," he laughs proudly at this.

"Oh, God. Poor Justin. I've got to get my hooks in him before you take all his money."

Paul grins. Mission accomplished. They pile into Jen's car and head to Sky Bar. The boys are already too drunk to drive. "We thought we could just hail a cab," they laugh to each other. Paul takes over the backseat, where he finds one of Jen's platform shoes. In her rearview mirror, she sees him holding it up to the headlights of the other cars.

"Your shoes are giving me a hard-on," he says.

"Oh, no," Jen gasps, "I hope there's enough room for you back there."

Max's song is playing in her head like a press release. To think, she might wind up having sex with a legendary penis! That would be one way to cut Max down to size.

"You are really *hurting* Paul," Justin says.

"You can bring those home if you want to," Jen says, grinning into the rearview mirror.

Inside Sky Bar, the three of them immediately lose one another. Jen heads to the bar by herself. She spots a shadowy-faced man across the room and stares at him for a moment. He looks familiar, probably an actor. She turns back to the bartender and holds out a twenty.

"Are you trying to avoid me?" a big voice says into her ear a minute later. She turns around to see the familiar man.

"Oh, God. Dean! I have got to get new lenses."

Dean is an entertainment lawyer. He's a black-haired former soccer player with a sensitive streak, and a wife. Jen worked with him on a project last month and they talked every day. Then, when they finally met for lunch two weeks ago, she couldn't eat. Every time she looked over at him, her mouth went dry and her throat closed. Afterward she called Nate and told him that Dean was the perfect unavailable man to break her of her Patrick standards. "I thought *I* was the perfect unavailable man," Nate said.

"Who are you here with?" Dean asks.

"I'm with these two guys from New York," she says searching the room for Justin and Paul.

"I feel as though I haven't talked to you in months. What are you working on now?"

She tells him about her latest project, a "millennium thriller." She is trying to figure out when she would have an excuse to call him again. He is probably the only man she knows who doesn't want anything from her.

While she is finishing her update, he grabs one of her arms and holds it out. "Look at those guns!" he says, staring at her naked arms. Jen glances at his hand on her biceps and blushes.

"Hey, Dean," two men say, approaching them. More lawyers, ready to talk deals.

Jen excuses herself to look for Justin and Paul. When she finds them, they are sitting in a booth, pupils dilated. They look as if they've swallowed a pack of pixie sticks. The bar is full of women who look like prom queens, parched blondes with bleached white teeth and plumped-up breasts, and they are overwhelmed by it all. Justin is quoting lines from a John Hughes prom movie, *Sixteen Candles,* jerking his head from side to side, pretending he is Anthony Michael Hall.

"Fresh breath is a priority in my life," he says, shaking his shoulders.

"Mom, Mom, I'm already wearing my headgear!" Jen says, offering up her favorite *Sixteen Candles* moment as she slides into the booth.

They both look up at her and laugh. "You're in the frat," Paul says, tipping his beer to her. She glances toward the bar for Dean and finally finds him, staring back at her. When the boys decide it's time to go, she tells them she'll meet them outside and runs back to Dean to say good-bye. "Call me!" he says gripping her hand.

She drives Paul and Justin back to their rental car. Paul jumps out first. Justin lingers in the front seat. He is staring into his lap, telling her a story, and his voice is getting lower. Oh, no. This is what happened at the Pleasure Palace three years ago, the night they kissed. "I'd love to hear about your project," he says. Jen is distracted and guarded. It just seems as if he is gearing up for another angle, the make-out route. She hikes up the pitch in her voice and wishes him luck with the rest of his trip. "Send me your script, Justin."

Justin presses his lips together and nods good-bye, staring at the sidewalk.

Anna

ANNA'S ANNUAL OFFICE party is in August. The whole world has slowed to a halt, and no one can get anything done, so the entire company leaves work early and heads to Elroy's, a big boisterous restaurant downtown. The entire company, that is, except Lizzie's group: they have been working overtime trying to finish this year's Thanksgiving stuffing campaign. The only thing worse than getting stuck on the stuffing account is getting stuck on the stuffing account in August.

Arriving at the restaurant, Anna heads to the bar, orders a vodka martini, and talks to Derek, the sexy assistant office manager with the distressed leather jacket and the squinty drunk eyes. She used to call him to order her bulletin board, hang her bulletin board, adjust her bulletin board, and get her a new cork-model bulletin board. He is actually a photographer, and this brings dignity to his work as her bulletin-board adjuster.

But now Derek is on his fourth bourbon and Anna can hardly understand him. She leaves him at the bar and makes her way around the restaurant, searching for Lizzie. She thinks she sees her friend Jeanne's brother, and she plunks herself affectionately onto his lap. She is about to plant one on his cheek when she jerks her head back and lets out a small shriek. "I have no idea who you are."

The man has his hands gripped firmly on her waist. "I'm practically giving this guy a lap dance," she laughs to the people watching. The man will not let her get up. She turns around and asks him what his name is. Then she looks down and shifts her weight. "I guess you won't be going anywhere soon," she says, standing up.

The guy's name is Spencer. He's friends with Ted, the quiet guy who works downstairs. Spencer is in the sixth hour of his thirty-fifth birthday celebration, and he thinks Anna is a present from one of his friends. This is probably not a good sign.

BY THE END of August, Anna and Spencer have run into each other at two after-work happy hours and one good-bye party, and they are now "involved." She calls after two weeks to report that the new man in her life is passing a series of tests. "He makes me pee," she says, which means he's funny enough. "He makes me feel young," which means he's older. "He's giving me room to get to like him," which means he's not around much.

Spencer's a lawyer for a white-shoe law firm, and he travels a lot for work. He gets his laundry done in Miami, buys a new pair of jeans in Quito, and sends Anna E-mails from Buenos Aires. "Back in S.F. next weekend . . . lap dancing on my yacht?"

Anna is heading to Chicago at the end of August to spend two weeks developing a campaign for a new client. She sends a note to Spencer with an invitation to her special performance, to be held, private screening, at the Drake Hotel. "It's where Oprah's guests stay," she writes.

"I'll be there," he responds the next day from Ecuador. Anna thinks he's kidding.

THE NIGHT AFTER Anna's first Chicago client meeting, Spencer is on his way to see her. She and Lizzie — who was sent to Chicago to help Anna's team with the market research for their new cereal account—have started in on their Drake Hotel minibar. Now they are mixing Johnnie Walker Red and Bailey's Irish Cream. What kind of guy flies fifteen hundred miles for a date? Anna wonders. He said he'd changed his business itinerary to spend the weekend with her and visit some old friends; he lived in Chicago for a while when he was a kid. Up until now, they've always been surrounded by familiar places, and cabs that can transport them quickly away from each other and back to their safe apartments. This time will be different.

Lizzie is pulling clothes out of Anna's suitcase. "You don't have a sex-date outfit," she is complaining. "We are going to have to go shopping. Is there a French Connection store in this city?"

Anna insists on jeans and a small white T-shirt. She can't bring herself to do the sex-date outfit. That first night, Spencer drags her all over the city in search of some friend of his, an actor, the "coolest guy" he knows. They are in the back of a cab, driving to another bar, when he points up to a stately building on Lake Shore Drive. "My parents have a place there," he says casually. "They never use it."

Throughout the night, Spencer offers up more indicators—his prep school, country club, the guys he went to Vanderbilt with. It all makes Anna a little uncomfortable. "He's not just from money, he's from old money," she says, anxious. "There are major differences between us. And he's definitely a conservative. The first question he asks anyone is, 'Where did you go to school?' Not 'What did you learn?' It's just not part of my code. I don't mind if they're rich now, but I hate it if their families are rich."

By the time they get back to the Drake, she is quiet.

"Hey," he says, when he notices this. "What happened to your straight-shooting trash talk?"

Anna is a management supervisor. She is a professional straight-shooter. She gets paid eighty thousand dollars a year to tell her clients exactly what she thinks. Sometimes this means trash-talking; profanity can be a powerful tool, she has learned. But now she is rummaging through her imagination for something to say. Nothing presents itself.

That night, she reports, they had "old boy" sex, the kind of sex they must teach in all-boy prep schools, the kind of sex that has made generations of them decide that women are "frigid." Anna is not the least bit ready when he digs for a condom. There is no ceremony with Spencer.

They take a walk along the lake to Lincoln Park the next morning. The water is a bright green-blue and the park smells of barbecues. Anna turns her face up to the sun.

"I have been doing so much traveling," Spencer says. "This job—I mean, forget about having a social life, much less starting a serious relationship."

Hmm. Anna's been doing a lot of traveling for her job, too, but he doesn't seem to notice. She turns to look at him and squints her eyes. "Is that supposed to be the surgeon general's warning?"

"No, no, I just . . ."

"No-o disclaimer needed" is all she says this time.

It's the infuriating first step in the demise of her sex drive. They were having a spontaneous fun weekend in a new city, and he immediately assumes she wants to marry him.

What it does, however, is buy them both some distance. He did fly nearly fifteen hundred miles for a date. A little scary. And he will just as quickly fly three thousand miles away to a safe distance.

ANNA SPENDS LABOR DAY weekend alone with her new client in Chicago. Spencer has left for Miami, and Lizzie had to fly back to San Francisco for another project. The client is based in Minneapolis, but she flew in to oversee the market research, and now she is relying on Anna to take her out each night. To make things worse, they are both staying at the Drake. "I have to spend every waking moment with the queen of bran flakes," Anna groans to Lizzie before she leaves.

By Saturday night, she has had it with the advertising talk and the wine menus and the mango-chutney-garnish restaurants. She takes her client to Mama's, a beer bar where Demi Moore took her friend in the movie *About Last Night*. Her client wears a red blazer and gold jewelery. She has not seen this movie Anna is talking about, and it's clear that this is not her kind of bar. Still, Anna buys them both Budweisers.

Three beers later, Anna has run out of small talk. "It's all about the king," she says, closing one eye and staring at the label of her beer, the king of beers, trying to distract herself from the boredom of her fourth night of client entertainment. These hours should be billable. A couple enters the bar and asks the bartender to turn up the TV. As the volume goes up, words flash at the bottom of the screen: Princess Diana Dead.

This can't be. She and Lizzie were just laughing about the latest *Star* headline: "DI ON SEX BINGE. 'I CAN'T GET ENOUGH!' " How can someone in the middle of a full-color supermarket sex binge just . . . die? And what will people read about in the full-cart check-out lane now?

People are closing in on them. They are pressed up against the bar as a roomful of Bud drinkers swarm in to stare at the screen.

After a half-hour of shock, Anna is struck by another terrible thought. Diana had to die the week before Anna's focus groups. "We are not going to get anyone to give up all of this death coverage for fifty dollars!" she tells her client.

"I know, I know," the client agrees. "We might as well take our vacations right now."

IF YOU'RE GOING to watch the funeral of the century, there is no better place than in a hotel, on an expense account. The following weekend, still holed up in the Drake after a week of sparse focus groups, Anna is preparing for the early-morning funeral. She orders a five A.M. wake-up call, dials up scrambled eggs, and loads the remote. "All I needed was a catheter and I would have made it straight through to *60 Minutes*."

Anna is captivated by the brother's brazen eulogy, especially the part about Diana's sons, William and Harry. He wants to make sure they are not immersed in duty and tradition, that they are free to experience "as many different aspects of life as possible to arm them spiritually and emotionally for the years ahead."

After the second broadcast of the funeral ceremony, she calls Gwen in Philadelphia, crying. "Promise me one thing?" she says blowing her nose into the receiver. "Promise me you won't let them talk about my battles with acne vulgaris?"

Gwen promises.

September

Let's face it. It's impossible to develop a
relationship in New York City. Everyone is
intimidated by the prospect of happiness.
They'd much rather suffer.

> —Thirty-nine-year-old woman,
>
> quoted in *New York* magazine

Jen

JEN IS TRYING to poke an earring stud into her left lobe. Mamie has just jumped, claws first, onto her shoulders. The phone is ringing. She hopes that maybe it's her date calling to cancel. This new woman at work set her up with some top-shelf executive, "way up on the Hollywood food chain," she said. Then she told Jen not to ask anyone about him. She wanted her to have an open mind. "So of course I commissioned an industrywide survey," Jen says. Turns out they call him "the professional dater." His last package was a blond girl from a WB Network show. Another one who's been dumped by a starlet. "This is not necessarily a bad thing," Emily reminds her. "He's been ego-tamed."

He called Jen the night before their date for a warm-up.

"So, what are you doing?" he asked.

"I'm out in my garden looking for coyotes. I'm afraid they're going to eat my cats."

Long pause. "How many cats do you have?"

"Is this a test question?"

"More than two and I'm hanging up."

"They're hanging from the rafters in there," Jen sighed.

"Are you smoking?"

"Is this test question two?"

"Not really."

"Just breathing."

"Heavy breathing?" he said, lowering his voice.

"Okay, we're going to have to save some things for our date. Besides, me and my nine cats have to go drag on some clove cigarettes."

A professional, no question, Jen thought when she hung up. A predate questionnaire! Doors are shutting in his face, which she can't yet picture. Still, she's been thinking about looking for another job. Her boss has been unbearable lately. She decided then that maybe this guy could hook her up with something.

She gives up on the earring and picks up the ringing phone.

"Do you remember this voice?" It's young and cute, but it's not ringing any bells.

"Uhh . . ."

"You have my gold slippers . . ."

"Hey!"

It's Patrick, and he waited until he had a job and an apartment to call again. They haven't spoken since the week after their big night. He wanted to show her he had grown up. He does seem older, except that his job is as an assistant and his apartment is in the Lower East Side and she is leaving to meet a mogul. Again with the timing. She spends ten minutes catching up with Patrick before she looks at her watch. "Oh, my God, I'm really late to meet a friend." She tells him to keep in touch.

She gives herself a pep talk on the drive to Bar Marmont. Focus, focus, focus. Emily called her this afternoon to remind her to stop looking at the door when she is on a date. "I can't help it. It's hard to turn that off," Jen told her. She has been conditioned to search for nearly thirty years, after all. Besides, how can anyone focus at Bar Marmont? There are bound to be distractions there. She never would have picked Bar Marmont.

Her date turns out to be kind of cute, in a beer-drinking college boy kind of way. He is jocky, no hair gel, but very smooth. They have a lot to talk about: he knows her boss, her boss's partner, her new friend down the hall. Maybe they have too much to talk about. She decides she has to be careful what she tells him. Still, she concentrates on keeping her shoulders locked in his direction, her eyes clamped on his, and her head bobbing with interest.

A famous TV actress approaches him with a big hug and a loud "How *are* you-u-u?" She starts rubbing his back. "Where have you *be-e-e-n?*" she says. After several minutes of this, she turns and makes a cute wave in Jen's direction, then leaves. Jen's date turns back to the table, unfazed, and touches Jen's arm. Without skipping a beat, he finishes his story. "So I decided to fly my dad to the set." Jen is trying to focus, but the actress is massaging another mini-mogul right behind them. She has to watch. The whole point of this is that people watch. Besides, her date hasn't stopped talking about himself, and she's kind of bored.

When the valet brings Jen's car, she leans over and gives her date a quick kiss good-bye. Then she almost sideswipes his Mercedes to avoid pulling up next to him at the first light. She waits until his car is out of sight and dials Becca's number on her car phone.

"I hope you are following him back to his bachelor pad," her sister says.

"Please, the guy's a professional dater."

"Did you do the eye-contact thing?"

"I did! I started to get into it. It's kind of like a game of chicken. You get sort of addicted."

"Was he really a pro?"

"Mm . . . a little too comfortable maybe. He was like this big jock trying to be confessional. He went off about his dad."

"He sounds charming."

"Yeah. I guess he was," Jen says, picturing him for a moment. "Guess who was there!"

Casey

THE WEEK AFTER her Labor Day weekend with Dave the sailing coach, Casey gets depressed. She can't walk down a block in New York without coming face-to-face with death. The newsstands are covered with it. First Princess Di, now Mother Teresa. The full spectrum of life and death. It doesn't help that summer is officially over. It's a little bit hard to take all at once.

She is watching a story on the paparazzi when Leo calls from Atlanta. They haven't spoken in three weeks, but he asks her when she is coming to visit. She is not sure if she can, she tells him. She is up for a promotion in November, and she has to prove she can handle the next level. Really, though, she is thinking that she should be saving what's left of her vacation days. Margot mentioned something about the family's annual sailing trip in the Florida Keys. She said that Dave booked a flight for a Jane Doe.

After she hangs up with Leo, she thinks about calling Dave. She still hasn't heard from him, and she wants to call Margot for advice but she can't. Meddlers would not be a good thing at this phase.

The Natalie Merchant concert is tonight, and Casey doesn't know if she is up for it. She can barely remember this Andrew guy, and there is a really good movie on TBS. Then he calls to tell her he has borrowed a friend's car and plans to pick her up at six. Now she has to go. She pulls a pair of jeans out of her laundry bag and grabs a windbreaker and meets him out on her corner. She is tired and trying not to yawn on the drive out there. Andrew is fair and blond, the opposite of Dave, and this is making it worse. But he skips the small talk and starts probing her with questions. He wants to know about her job: what she does each day, what she likes about it, what she doesn't like about it, where she wants to end up. He wants to know what she thinks about things—the entertainment business, where it's going, what she thinks of "misogyny rock." They don't stop talking until halfway through the concert, when rows of arms in front of them shoot up at once, pointing to a shooting star. When he pulls up to her block two hours later, she leans over and carefully kisses him good-bye.

Back in her apartment, she fishes around in her appointment book until she finds Dave's E-mail address. She completely lost herself, disappeared into her date, and it somehow feels like a betrayal. The weekend with Dave seemed so serious—a courtship. And Dave's the perfect man, the perfect coach-man. She sends him a short note from work the next morning. "How's Memphis? Are you coming back for a break?"

After three days go by and nothing comes back to her, Casey starts to sulk. "I was starting to think he was the payoff for all the bad starts. How does he know I'm not going to fall for someone else? I would have waited, but now I just can't."

*   *   *

PEOPLE IN THE music business can't take a summer vacation until all the concertgoers are back in school. For their September holiday, Casey and her friend Maggie have planned a tour of southern Utah and the Grand Canyon. Maggie had a two-for-one plane ticket and they wanted to go to the cheapest place they could find that was still interesting, so they decided on the wild land formations of Utah. "Every place in the world is exactly the same right now — Starbucks, Gap, McDonald's," Casey explains. "The Grand Canyon is the last frontier."

She has carefully mapped out their itinerary with a Mobil travel guide and a Fodor's. There's been too much clutter lately, she says, too much work, too many men in her life. She wants to live simply, bonding with nature and her best cowgirl friend. Plus, "New York City can make you a little soft," she explains. "You have to toughen yourself up every so often."

At the car rental agency in the Las Vegas airport, Casey and Maggie are upgraded to preferred customers and given the keys to a green convertible. "That is the first sign," she says. "We were not in Manhattan anymore." They pop a mixed tape into the dashboard, tie their hair back, and drive at ninety miles an hour to Moab, a mountain-biking mecca and the first stop on their tour. Roaming the microbreweries that night, they quickly attract new clutter: "The men were all over us. They're used to families. It was as if they hadn't seen anything like us for years." Still, Casey and Maggie stay focused. They have to get up early the next day and drive to Zion National Park. There are horses to ride, there is whitewater to raft.

After spending a rough day river rafting, tanned and covered in bruises, they head for the Green Valley hot springs, where they meet a long-haired trust-fund hippie named Oliver. He massages their feet and tells Casey about his problems with his dad. He also mentions a friend in New York who just started a ginseng supply company, someone he wants her to meet. Before she leaves, he gives her a chunk of purple quartz, and they exchange phone numbers.

The next day, Casey and Maggie head to the Bright Angel Lodge at the Grand Canyon, where they ride horses along the canyon rim, taking pictures of each other in their saddles in front of the last Gap-less stretch of America. That night over dinner they meet the lodge's chef. He looks like Michael Stipe on steroids—big whiskery eyes, a sullen mouth, and arms cut out of glacial rock. He talks to them throughout their dinner about the constellations and sunset photography and his spinach frittata. Casey devours her plate. The next morning, he tries to surprise them by delivering coffee to their room, but instead wakes up an older Japanese couple. In lieu of the coffee, he cooks them a special soufflé for dinner and invites Casey down to his suite. He tells her about his dreams of becoming a rafting guide, and then he starts kissing her.

"You are just going to forget about me," he says, interrupting their kiss.

"How can you say that?" she says, one hand on his stomach. They spend half the night together, but Casey is reluctant to let things get too far. "I felt like a horrible guy. I was going to abandon him in the morning." Then she decided that she would be more horrible if she ruined their perfect night together. "He was very enthusiastic. I didn't want to squash that. I don't think he has many opportunities."

On the drive back to Moab, Casey cannot stop smiling. "This is the best trip," she screams to Maggie over the blaring mixed tape. Maggie spent the night on the phone with her boyfriend back in New York.

"Why are men in New York so neurotic?" Maggie yells.

"I don't know. But we've got to tell everyone to get out and see the other side!"

They stop at a Circle K gas station. Casey gets out to clean her window, and a man with long brown hair and black sunglasses, filling his gas tank in front of her, looks up and smiles. "Where you girls off to?" he asks her.

"We're heading back to Moab," she says, shading her eyes.

"I'm heading there myself in a couple of days," he says. "Maybe we can meet up."

"That'd be great," she says, knowing that she'll be gone by then. They exchange home numbers at the cash register.

"Leave a message on my machine telling me where you'll be," he says. She sticks his number in her knapsack pouch, with the others.

IT'S SUNDAY WHEN Casey gets back to New York. The first thing she notices about her apartment is the answering machine, which isn't blinking. Granted, she called in for messages from the Las Vegas airport, but she thought someone would have welcomed her back. She drops her stuff by the door and curls up on the couch. What now? Her crazy work summer is over. Her big trip is over. Her men are all over. What *now*?

She walks down to the neighborhood stationery store and buys herself a new journal. She is going to lose herself in the tales of her western adventures. She'll write about what it felt like to be out there, and the people she met, so unlike anyone she knows in New York. She sits down to write about the Bright Angel Lodge when the phone rings. "Remember me?" the gas station man says from a pay phone. "I missed you in Moab."

Casey calls to report in as soon as she hangs up. "I get nothing from Dave. Nothing from Andrew. Not even a message from Stefan. But the gas station guy, he's got class. These New York guys, they are not cooperating."

Anna

SAN FRANCISCO IS bracing for El Niño, Chelsea Clinton's arrival at Stanford, and "emotional intelligence" classes in the schools. Back in her office, Anna is bracing for the bran flakes campaign. She has left her bag half-packed for her next trip, which is emotionally intelligent. She will most likely have to travel again in the next two weeks, and she is in touch with how exhausting this can be.

Spencer is now in Mexico City, under the smog, where he belongs. She has decided to make him a satellite office in the orbit of her mind, a vendor to contract out to for special services. "It was pretty clear by the end of our Chicago weekend that we weren't going anywhere. There was no need to have a conversation about it. I think it was understood that we were just going to let it take its course."

And, really, she's been too busy with work to focus on it. In addition to the cereal account, she is now working on a new campaign for a coffee client, and she is developing a special relationship with caffeine. Caffeine is far more stimulating than Spencer, she decides. She contemplates this concept as a campaign strategy.

One of the women on the account, a group supervisor from downstairs, has invited Anna to her wedding shower. Anna is clearly a B-list guest, a work protocol thing, and she's not especially eager to attend. Come to think of it, she has never been excited about wedding showers, not even her own. To top it all off, the bride-to-be and her fiancé just moved into a three-story town house in Pacific Heights with a strikingly steep view of the bay. Anna is suddenly aware that her thirty-dollar present, to be so very publicly opened and discussed in an hour, will not compete.

She forces herself to go anyway, and arrives just in time for an icebreaker quiz to warm things up: "Where did Alexis and Bartholomew go on their first date?" someone reads from a slip of paper. Anna had no idea the guy's name was Bartholomew, but this makes sense, she decides. She offers to write down the gifts.

The women fall silent when the gift ceremony begins. A junior account executive didn't know that she was supposed to wrap her gift in a big bow for the special "bow hat"—a contraption of stapled ribbons that is supposed to bring the bride-to-be lots of babies. The college roommate didn't know that the groom's mother would be there, and she is trying to hide her Kinky Kitty bag. The twenty-six-year-old account executives who are stuck paying eight-hundred-dollar rents by themselves are wondering why they have to buy two gifts for their already wealthy boss, who now gets to double her income and split her rent. The laughter is strained.

Anna wonders if everyone is in as bad a mood as she is on the drive home. "I want to get married so they'll do one of those quizzes for me," she announces to Lizzie and Jeanne in the car. "Does Anna prefer anal sex or group sex? Mrs. O'Denehy?"

Later that night, Anna and Lizzie drive to the Mission to meet Ted and Derek, friends from work. Ted and Lizzie got together the night of the office party at Elroy's and are still at that early phase where they need "date company." Derek is the sexy assistant office manager who just put in notice. He's moving to Wisconsin to be with his girlfriend. "Derek does have that something," Lizzie says on the ride over. "Except that he's lilly." Lilly means lilliputian, after the little people in *Gulliver's Travels*, and it is their word for men whose jeans they can't wear. If you can't fit into his 501's, then he is too lilly to love.

They meet Ted and Derek at the Make Out Room, an old high-ceilinged saloon that is draped in dark-red velvet and lit with strings of colored Christmas lights. Two elk heads hang from above a dark oak bar, one with his nose cupped in a bra. Derek, chewing on a cigarette, is talking to a redhead in the back room. He's wearing his scratched leather jacket and heroin addict hair—half matted, half spiked. Ted sits alone on a bar stool.

Anna and Lizzie pull up stools next to Ted, and soon Derek joins them. They talk about the new president at work and the rules that were posted in the rec room. When they run out of common denominators, Derek starts telling stories about Africa. "I was living in Botswana with this woman who worked in the Peace Corps," he is saying. "Then one day I came home and she was gone." He twists his mouth to exhale smoke. "The bitch ran off to Seattle with a lawyer." The women stare at him as if in a trance. Ted is wincing. He's been in the shadow of guys like Derek before.

They leave when the Make Out Room starts to fill up and walk up Valencia Street to the Lone Palm. The men here look as though they've been cast to play Tori Spelling's latest love interest: sunken eyes, furrowed foreheads. The Mission is full of moody lounge bars with cynical effects: a Madame Alexander doll hanging upside down from her plastic toe, a Buddha in a manger, a blinding blue neon frame, red crinkled patio candles. It's intimidating. Then you see the pool table in the corner, the yellow dreadlocks hanging over a cue stick, the undergarment clinging to an elk nostril. The bar was concocted by a couple of Stanford students on mushrooms.

Now Derek is talking about his current girlfriend, who just left to start a job in Wisconsin. He believes in "letting people loose," which means he has been fooling around since she left, even though he is planning to move in with her in a month. "She wouldn't want me to just be dead, hanging my head low, getting drunk by myself. She'd want me to be a live wire, full of . . . verve." He takes a squinty drag on his cigarette.

"And what about her?" Lizzie asks, one eyebrow cocked.

"I want her to live, too. I want her to be experiencing life. I don't want her . . ." he drops his head and plows his hand through his hair, sweeping it into a pompadoured drift.

"Running off with a lawyer like the bitch?" Ted says.

The women start to laugh, then stop.

Outside on Seventeenth Street, Derek pulls Anna back behind the others. He stops on the sidewalk and plows his hair again; he is trying to speak. "I don't know what it is," he says finally, "but I think I need to kiss you."

Anna stares at Lizzie and Ted as they move away from her, and she shifts her weight from hip to hip. She is trying to imagine verve. She is trying to picture live wires.

"I'll tell you what," she says. "We'll go out next week."

October

I actually like the quest. The more lost you
are, the more you have to look forward to.
What do you know, I'm having a great time
and I don't even know it.

—Ally McBeal

"I QUIT," Jen calls to announce halfway into October. She sounds as though she's hyperventilating. "I just quit. Told him I couldn't take it anymore. He came in screaming holy hell again, so I told him he's on his own. Then I packed up my things and left."

The first two days are terrible. She is afraid she has made a big mistake. Her brother-in-law said she should not have quit until she had another job lined up, and now she can't sleep. She is afraid, mostly, that she will have no friends. No social life. No point. No one is waiting for her, she says, chain-smoking and coughing into the phone one night. No one is even yelling at her. It's terrifying. She was sitting in the vortex of *something*—and now, nothing. She can't even think about her credit card. She will have to cash in her emergency savings.

The second week is better. She discovers that she has sacked away three months' worth of savings, which buys her time. Word is out, and people are calling with job offers. People are even calling to congratulate her. "You have balls, woman!" Emily tells her. Jen decides to take some time to figure out what she is going to do next.

After a few days, she falls into a new pattern: she sleeps in, rides her bike along the Santa Monica boardwalk, and meets people for lunch. She scratches Rudy and Mamie. Her breathing returns to normal. Other parts of her surface. She remembers what it's like to read whatever she wants to read. She remembers what it's like to sleep through the night without a plunging anxiety attack. She remembers what it's like not to fear the phone. And then it happens—her sex drive comes back. Out of nowhere. And she has no outlets.

She makes an appointment at a day spa in Santa Monica. A sex substitute. Expensive safe sex, with exfoliation. And no messy emotions. Just emollients. Jen decides unemployment could be fun.

After her massage, she calls Fiona from her car. "I want to be a Hollywood wife," she announces.

"Except that you have a thing for Hollywood husbands," Fiona tells her.

"I know. Parasites. They all want to live off of me. Or at least they did. I haven't heard from any of them, not even James."

"Well, this is one way to shake them." Fiona tries to reassure her.

"It's about being by yourself."

"What is?"

"The Hollywood wife thing. You marry a mogul, and he's never home. You go to a couple of functions together, wear a great dress. Then you spend the rest of your time alone. No awful bosses. No annoying phone calls you have to take," Jen says.

"I can't believe I am hearing this from you. Two more weeks of this and you'll be climbing the walls."

"Uh-uh. I'll be a home economist. And instead of working, I'll get work done—mannies, peddies, glycolic acid facials . . ."

People keep coming up with different ideas for what Jen should do next. Dean the lawyer wants her to come work for him. Her friend Stewart wants her to help start a magazine. Emily from work thinks she should work on a new Fox show, *Ally McBeal,* which takes place in Boston. Evan the ex thinks she should come to New York. She listens enthusiastically to each suggestion. Then she books another appointment at the spa.

After two more weeks, Jen starts making lists. Then she starts making lists of lists. "People to call list." "Jobs to look into list." She is spinning in the possibilities of it all. She could be anything, after all. She could live anywhere: New York, London, L.A. Maybe not anywhere. She is starting to think she should just be an independent. An independent producer. This way she can plug herself in and out of projects, and she doesn't have to commit to any one job. She can still splash around in the possibility of everything.

KATE'S BIRTHDAY PARTY is the third week in October—Jen's first big public outing since she left her job. She is a little nervous. She has never been to a party in L.A. without a job. She's not sure what people will talk to her about.

The party is being thrown by Kate's new boyfriend, Roger, at his house in Eagle Rock. Kate is a movie costume designer, so the party promises to be a runway show. Becca chooses an L.A. grunge look for the evening—wide waling, hip-hugging, clam-shucking pants and platform Birkenstocks, smelly Berkeley shoes with perfectly pedicured slate-blue toenails. Her husband, Alex, has on his Potsy sweater—a cool wool zip-up with vertical stripes. Jen is wearing a new vintage dress, which is mostly covered up by a long suede jacket. Hard as Becca has tried, her little sister still can't seem to shed her puritanical New England roots.

Becca and Alex give Kate a membership to Trashy Lingerie, a special wallet-sized club card that must be flashed before entering the "private" store. Kate's boyfriend, Roger, an approved member, found her her favorite dress there, a leopard-skin slip dress with a plunging neckline. He bought it for a premiere that she never made it to. Roger tackled her as she was sliding into her shoes, and they never made it out the door.

Nate is there. In wallflower mode. Things fell apart with the rock goddess over the summer, and last month, when his sentences started to trail off, Jen told him to get help. Now he's on Zoloft, and his sentences never end. Instead of actually *being* depressed, he talks wistfully about depression. He has cornered Jen by the bathroom. "It's just that, New York has an edge to it. It is so *real*," he is telling her. "L.A. is just a big strip mall, and the sun shines too damn much." After about twenty minutes, Nate gets to the point. "You can't drink here. You have to drive everywhere. I'm not interesting when I don't drink."

The thing is, Jen doesn't mind Nate so much lately. He provides welcome shade in what *can* be a too-bright city. Besides, he hasn't abandoned her just because she quit her job.

Still, her sister and brother-in-law are on rescue alert. Becca does not like the fact that Jen traps herself with social work cases. She sends Alex over. He grabs Jen's hand and pulls her to his chest. "Will you be Potsy's date?" he asks. This is a cue. Jen flattens her head against Alex's shoulder while he drags her, feet dangling, around the living room. This is the Potsy dance.

A group of women standing around the nachos are watching them. "He was a five-foot-high pompadoured fink!" one of them says, loudly enough for Jen to hear. She is talking about Fonzi.

"He was a *slut*," another one adds, cornering a chunk of salsa. "The man had a ménage-à-trois every night!"

"To think our taste in men was dictated by Aaron Spelling."

"Is that why I'm only attracted to short men?"

"Mmm. And they're all holding out for Barbara Eden." The woman props her breasts up with folded arms. " 'If you say so, Master!' "

Two sleek-headed Vince Vaughn stunt doubles are hovering near the nachos. Decked in cocktail clothes, oversized collars, and bowling shoes, they are discussing the Dresden, the bar from the movie *Swingers*. "That place has lost its quotient hipness," one of the women tells them, and she is not just being smug. Jen knows that she calculates hip quotients for a living. A big living. She plugs in numbers — box office draw, magazine cover sales, tabloid scandals — and assigns values to properties based on their hip quotient. Drew Barrymore? Jen asked her once. She's about an 8.3. Bankable. When she says the Dresden has lost its hip quotient, she is doing the math.

Finished with her Potsy dance, Jen is reminded that Max's wedding is tonight, something she had forgotten until Kate introduces her to a stringy-haired acoustic guitarist. His band played at Spaceland last week, he tells her. About twenty-four, he's dressed in green sneakers and knee-length shorts. He looks as if he has the soul of a thirteen-year-old skateboard punk on Venice Beach.

The nacho women have moved on to the cupcakes and a new

topic. Men and women both play by "rules," a Fonzi analyst is saying. It's the same rules they teach sales reps. "You make a pitch, then you back off. You have to give people the space to make the affirmative move."

"I think it's about buying time," her salsa friend says. "People have to sift out the 'it' from the 'them.' Everyone wants the 'it': sex, security, drama, falling in love, a sperm donor. But you have to separate that from the person. You're not going to know if it's about the person right away. So you hedge."

Jen is lingering near the cupcakes, listening. She is thinking about the dater—she never heard from him again. At first she didn't really want to hear from him, but yesterday she was thinking about how he made her laugh and how attentively he touched her arms. She pulls an M&M off of a cupcake and decides that the dater was definitely about the "it." She is missing many its.

She decides to find Becca and Alex and ask them when they will be ready to leave. They are talking to Kate about the beautiful two-story Tudor they have been fixing up. It has a sunken living room, a sunroom, and several small gardens. They are thinking about having a baby. Becca asks Jen if she will come over Sunday and help her weed the garden. "You have *got* to be kidding," Jen says with a scowl.

Just before they are about to leave, Dean the lawyer arrives, date-less. He works with Roger. Jen hasn't seen him since they ran into each other at Sky Bar in August. "Hey!" he says, kissing Jen on the cheek. "Roger said you might be here." Jen turns to Becca and begs her to stay. "What are you *thinking?*" Becca whispers, a vein popping out of her neck.

Becca convinces Jen that they should leave, and as they go to find Alex, Dean comes up from behind and grabs Jen's arms. "Hey, you," he says. "I've missed you." Jen laughs nervously.

"What are you *thinking?*" Becca says again on the ride home. "He's *married.*"

THE PROMISE KEEPERS are storming Washington, hundreds of thousands of burly lost men begging forgiveness for breaking promises and abandoning their children. No women are invited. Women interfere with "a man's immediate soul-searching," according to the group's spokesman.

Ethan is a "promise keeper," Anna decides when she reads about this in the *San Francisco Chronicle*. He has kept his promise to be a father to his current ex-girlfriend's future baby. His current ex-girlfriend is invited, however, to partake in his immediate soul-searching. What kind of promise keeper sticks with the interfering woman?

Anna is keeping her own promises, meeting her old college friend Ness at a French café on a side street near Union Square. Ness wants to show Anna the photos from their trip to Aspen, and Anna wants to help Ness put together a marketing plan for her new design business. Ness and her husband take care of Anna; they cook her dinner, do her taxes, feed her cat, cheer her up. She is always struggling to come up with something she can do in return, but they never seem to need anything. When they were just out of college, she used to stay up late giving Ness relationship advice, pulling the phone into the living room so that Greg wouldn't hear. Ness doesn't exactly need that anymore, so Anna was thrilled when Ness mentioned the marketing plan.

They grab an outdoor table, order a fruit and cheese platter, and begin drafting an outline together, stopping every few minutes to stare out at the other tables. Anna spots a woman who looks just like their friend Alison.

"I wish all our friends lived here," she says.

"That reminds me," Ness says. "We all owe sixty dollars for Gary and Alison's wedding present."

Anna wrinkles her forehead. "How can I owe sixty dollars?"

"It came to two hundred forty dollars total," Ness says, making a fist and dropping a finger for each of the gift participants: "Me and John" (index finger), "Christina and Scott" (middle finger), "Carmen and Josh" (ring finger), "Anna" (pinky).

Now Anna is pouting. "I'm being punished for not getting laid."

Ness drops Anna's share down to thirty dollars. When they are finished sketching out their proposal, Anna starts to tell Ness about Derek, the sexy assistant office manager, and the kiss on the sidewalk.

"Is this the heroin addict who hooked up your computer at work?" Ness asks.

Anna's dating stories make Ness uneasy. She doesn't remember anything particularly exciting about being single, and she looks at Anna with a hint of concern.

"He's not a heroin addict," Anna says.

"He crashed the entire company network when he plugged in your computer."

"He's a photographer. He's not a computer geek."

Ness teases Anna that she is in the middle of some kind of savior trip, the stifled mommy in her trying to save all the troubled teenagers.

"This is not true," Anna insists. "I am actually looking for someone to save me. A tall, handsome dermatologist, ready to rescue my aging epidermis."

Anna envies Ness sometimes. But she was Ness once. The problem with Ness is that her life is a screenplay we already know the ending to. She's done. She met the guy, is living happily ever after, The End. This doesn't mean we won't rent the video every now and then—her life is comforting. But Anna is not entirely sure she wants to be done.

THE FOLLOWING WEEK Anna reads an E-mail from Derek. "I'm taking you to Moxie," it says. "Eight o'clock tomorrow night." Moxie is an expensive Eastern European restaurant.

"Where did you come up with Moxie?" she E-mails back. "And who's paying?"

"Sara recommended it," he responds an hour later. Sara is Derek's former boss. She quit to move to Napa Valley to start an olive oil business. "Sara says I should pay. She thinks we should sleep together."

Anna's breathing gets quicker. He's online. She has to think of a response fast, or he'll think she's choking.

"This from a woman who squooshes olives?" Anna types back.

ANNA IS TWENTY minutes late for their dinner. Derek is waiting on the street in his distressed leather jacket, one hand on the back of his head. He tells her he's a little nervous, and that he needs to "slam down a couple of drinks." ("It was so damn cute," she says when she recounts the tale, then pauses. "Listen to me. Alcoholism is so-o cu-u-te.")

He had some trouble warming up to the dinner part, too, she reports. He felt a little "on the spot," he told her. "Okay, he's a bit of a freak. But he's a good freak. A good funny freak. He's a little curious, and he's clearly exploring the edges. He talked about West African literature. I think he was making it all up."

Derek is actually from a small clean town outside Seattle, but he has a lot on his mind. He had an abnormal childhood in an entirely normal town, and he is caught up in his contrasts. "He had a radical mother and, like, a military father or something. He's interesting . . . okay, confused, but he makes me think differently."

After dinner, they walk around the Mission for a half-hour, talking about how they grew up and wondering if they will ever feel settled. Then he stops her on the sidewalk again. "I'm really attracted to you," he says in his smoky voice, "and I want to be with you. But you need to know something. I am moving to Wisconsin to be with this woman. Does it bother you?" Here we go again with the honesty.

"Well, I'm not in love with the idea that you're in love with someone," Anna responds. "But I understand. I like you and I'm attracted to you, but I'm confused too . . ."

Later Anna admits: "Okay, it was a little unsettling. But he's interesting and he's pushing my buttons. I decide, okay, I'm going to do it. It's a no-brainer. I'll get my head around it later."

She spends the night at his place in the Mission. "I was expecting edgy, but he was much more sweet. Before we even start kissing, he opens up his top drawer and pulls out a pair of L. L. Bean pajamas for me."

His alarm goes off at six the next morning, L. L. Bean pajamas scattered across the room. They didn't fall asleep until around four. They spent half the night rolling around, then lost their nerve when it came time to finish their "assignment." "I think we just talked about everything too much," Anna speculates. And then they spent an hour and a half talking about everything even more. It seems Derek was not as *loose* as his girlfriend allegedly wanted him to be.

It's a Wednesday morning and he lives in a creepy rundown neighborhood, and Anna can't get a cab. She yells up to his window and tells him to call one for her.

When the cab finally comes, the driver starts yelling at her. "What-are-you doing here? Terrible neighborhood, young girl . . ." Anna tells the man she was simply staying at her boyfriend's apartment. She has to go home now and go to her job in advertising.

"This is bad. *Boyfriend.* Now I'm lying to a cabbie."

Sitting in front of her computer four hours later, she gets an E-mail from Derek. "I feel great today," it says. She grins at her blue screen. She gave good . . . verve. A half-hour later she gets another E-mail, and this one's from Spencer. He's back from Europe and wants to know if she's around this weekend. There's a Halloween party at a house in Noe Valley.

Spencer? Anna had forgotten about Spencer. She is getting better and better at this, forgetting people. Each one squeezes out the next. Staring at the E-mail, she decides she sort of misses him. She calls Lizzie and tells her to come up with an outfit for Halloween.

RESTAURANT NIPPON USED to be Casey's favorite. It's where all the big Japanese executives go for sushi. Stefan has ordered them both the salmon roll. It's the first time Casey has seen him in two months, but it feels longer. They don't seem to have that much to talk about anymore. He told her last month that his divorce is on hold; his wife still lives in California, and he doesn't want to pay the fifty percent alimony.

Now is really not a good time to be the other woman. You could be sued, for one thing. Or you could be dishonorably discharged. Worst of all, you could end up being *the* woman. Terrifying.

After the third round of sakè, it hits her. They didn't fall in love over sushi, they fell in love over sakè. She had her sakè goggles on. She starts quietly doing breathing exercises, bloating out her stomach under the table to the silent count of ten. What if he asks her to go home with him? She has been trying to turn this back into a friendship, but she's worried. What if he gets mad at her? She doesn't want a big scene. What if he starts saying bad things about her to people at work? Before the check comes, he pats his mouth with his napkin and tells Casey he has a headache and has to go home.

In the cab back down to her apartment, Casey feels herself backsliding again. She presses her fingers up against the windowpane and drags them down the glass. Then she starts flipping through the Rolodex of men she keeps in her mind, trying to flop to one she can land on, a distraction, a plan. Dave the sailor? He never responded to her E-mail. She keeps flipping. Andrew the guy from the Natalie Merchant concert? He went away on some big reporting assignment. Flip, flip, flip. Fletcher?

Casey has known Fletcher for eight years. He's an aging musician who played in a few big bands in the eighties and lives five blocks away on a burgundy-brownstone street. She first met him out with friends one night, and for reasons she still doesn't understand, she couldn't stop staring at him. But she had a boyfriend then, and Fletcher was a musician. Casey has a carefully thought-out policy about dating musicians:

"I find that the male ego is complex enough. To infuse it with the artist ego, well, I don't have enough time. I have too many needs of my own to look after that male artist ego. I'm sorry. I might change my mind one day. But when it comes to musicians, you're dealing with the Peter Pan problem, and a built-in promiscuity that I just won't tolerate. Maybe some people will. But talking yourself out of jealousy is an exhausting process. If you get involved with a guy who's out on the road with women throwing themselves at him . . . I can't do that. I can trust for only so long. I just think they're a bad bet. And even though they're sexy, they're just too needy. I need someone strong."

But then Casey ran into Fletcher in her neighborhood last week, and he told her he had just had a dream about her. It's not as though he's a young, smoldering rock star, she thought, listening to him talk about his dream. Then she had an epiphany. "I looked at him and thought—this guy is going to be my next lover."

He called the following week, and they split a bottle of wine at a small basement restaurant near his apartment, the kind you have to step down into. Then they went home together. "We had the same agenda," she says. "Neighborhood sex. It was very cozy."

Now she has an extra pass to the VH1 Fashion Awards party at Chelsea Piers, and she is debating whether to bring him. There will be a lot of work people there he will know. But there will also be lots of new people to meet, and faces to gawk at. She decides to go alone.

Dressed in a pair of shiny blue hip-huggers, Casey spends the first hour making the record rounds. Everyone is distracted. The people in the music business are very sloppy. They are not used to all these creatures—pasted and perfected and towering over them. She drifts around the room, taking in all the colors. Then she spots Beth and two guys from work on the dance floor and joins in. People are spilling martinis on their outfits. It suddenly occurs to her that she will be going home alone, too. "You can't go home from a wild party alone," she explains later. She ends up trekking to the pay phones to call Fletcher and invite him to meet her there at midnight.

Casey and Fletcher have B-plus sex. "It's pretty good, probably because the pressure is off. It feels a little funny, the casual sex thing. But it's a release of energy. And if you can't be anchored with serious feelings, at least you can have a solid friendship."

Fletcher picks up on Casey's pragmatic approach to their relationship. Sometimes he feels like the emotional equivalent of a lotus position. He tries to joke the next morning that she is just using him for his body.

"I don't really know where he got this from," she reports in after he leaves. "It's not as though I talked about other guys. And, really, if it was just about the body, I would have flown in the Canyon chef."

CASEY WAKES AT seven A.M. Halloween morning with a phone call from her mother. Early-morning phone calls are never good, and this one is no exception. Her grandmother has died. She had been sick for a while, but Casey is struck by the news. Adults are not usually allowed much in the way of mourning when it comes to grandparents, but Casey decides she needs the day off from work. "I really admired this woman. So much of me I get from her. My personality. My middle name. She was a flapper, and she was sporty before her time."

It's Halloween, and everyone is walking around her Greenwich Village neighborhood rejoicing in morbidity and transgender dressing. All of it makes Casey sad. She can't even flip through her mental Rolodex. She goes to yoga class and lies on her mat and stares up at the ceiling. She could have provided a ten-year-old great-granddaughter by now.

The message light is beating rapidly when Casey gets home. Stefan has called to offer condolences. He heard about her grandmother from a colleague. Andrew the reporter is back from a four-week assignment and wants to know if she's free for drinks. And a guy named Randy—"you met my friend Oliver at the hot springs in Utah"—also wants to meet for a drink. She heads uptown to meet Andrew in his neighborhood. He is full of stories and questions, and he is making her laugh. He asks her about her grandmother, her parents, her yoga class. He manages to poke through her sadness. When he gets up to go to the bathroom, she watches him cross the room, then stares at his empty drink. She is so impressed with him. He's a shrink who doesn't even ask for money. He comes back to the table and announces that he has to catch an early flight. They end the night with a hailed-taxi kiss.

They say you should never start something when you're sad, when you are empty. There's a risk that you will fill yourself up with a person and lose your equilibrium, lose sight of yourself. Casey doesn't know what to make of Andrew. She is afraid she will fill up with him, lose herself in his stories and his ice cubes.

The next night Casey meets Fletcher at Tramps. An R&B act is playing. She is standing at the café bar with Fletcher when she spots a talent scout she had a crush on several years ago. The scout stops her on her way to the bathroom a half-hour later. "Don't tell me you're with *Fletcher*," the man whispers into Casey's hair. She doesn't like this. Fletcher has probably been sucking up to this guy for over a decade, and this makes her queasy. She knows how insecure Fletcher can get, his fragile "artist" ego, and yet she knows how awful it is to be "hustled," and it's hard to decide whom to root for here.

What's making it worse is that she's not sure if she can go home with Fletcher again. She is still sad about her grandmother. And she keeps thinking about Andrew. Besides, the sex has been sliding down the grade curve, and her yoga instructor said that she should be careful about how she spends her energy. C-minus sex can be a bad use of energy.

But Fletcher is an insecure musician, and the talent scout guy was so damn smug. She ends up back at his apartment a few hours later. They are just getting things started when she feels a piercing pain on her waist. "Ow!" she yells. "You *bit* me."

Fletcher grins. Casey checks to see if he broke the skin.

"You bit me hard. Why did you do that?"

"Because you're mean," he says. "All you bitches are the same. You're mean."

Fletcher tells her he is just being playful, downtown-guy playful, but Casey doesn't like it. Her cozy fragile neighborhood date has just turned.

Jen

THE STOCK MARKET just hit a new high. The unemployment rate is getting even lower. According to *U.S. News & World Report*, even Gen-Xers are saving and investing piles of cash. Jen is starting to eye her jar of quarters nervously. Still looking for a job, she is getting restless. She has been holding out for something that she can commit to, and so far there's nothing, so she's been living on her savings and credit cards. Meanwhile, everyone else seems to be in the grind of work, and the only steady calls she gets are from Becca and the unemployed ponytailed screenwriter. He's become her personal stalker, which is fine for now, because she can't afford a personal trainer and she could use the attention.

She could also use some excitement, and she's been thinking about calling the professional dater. He didn't call after their date, but then, she didn't exactly send any signals, and she could have followed up and called him. She decides to consult her brother-in-law for advice. "I liked the dater, Alex," she tells him one boring Wednesday. "We hit it off. I don't get why he didn't call."

"Look, Jen, the guy's a status dater. A label fucker. You've lost your label. You don't want some guy who just wants your business card in his Rolodex." Jen suddenly wishes she were fifteen, listening to Becca tell her that Billy Bernard was just trying to get to third base. There was something pure and flattering about that.

Lately she has been remembering her lost past fondly — her dates, her job, the people at work, even her boss. It's almost maudlin. She calls Emily at the office. They used to have so much fun together at work.

"I am so fuck-*ing pissed,*" Emily says when she hears Jen's voice. An ex-boyfriend, the guy down the hall, threw a party and didn't invite her, even though she has invited him to hers. His new girl-friend couldn't deal with any exes. "With each guy I've dated, I've been pushed farther and farther out of the boys' club." Somehow this makes Jen feel better. Even if she had a job, she would still be on the outside looking in.

She turns on *The View*—the new daytime talk show created by Barbara Walters with lots of professional women sitting around a living room talking. Jen decides she should be getting paid to do this and makes a note to write Barbara a letter. Today they are talking about a memory enhancer. Jen is going to suggest they do a story about memory reducers. Hasn't anyone invented a memory blocker yet? There's got to be a vitamin that blocks out everything you liked about your previous life.

The next day, Jen is in her pajamas reading magazines when Becca calls with a plan. Her friend Gabby is working on the set of a film somewhere in England and has invited Becca to visit. Becca begs Jen to come with her. In less than two months, Jen will most likely be back in some office, pressing buttons, getting yelled at, Becca reminds her. This is her last chance to take a real vacation.

They fly into London, rent a stubby Peugeot, and take turns driving to the English countryside. The first hour is hairy. They are not used to driving on the left side of the road and they are both yelling at each other, gripping their doors. Jen tries to break the tension by remembering songs they used to sing on trips with their parents. She sings the words to a Beach Boys song, the one about the Midwest farmers' daughters and how they make you feel all right. Becca tries to finish the verse with a line about east coast girls, but she starts humming halfway through it.

"I can't believe you still don't know the words to that song," Jen says, staring over at her big sister.

"Will you *watch* the *road!*" Becca yells, practically standing in her seat.

Jen tries again. "Remember when we made up that jingle for the Famous Amos cookie contest? We were convinced we were going to win."

"We were jumping up and down when they were getting ready to announce it on the radio."

"It never occurred to either of us we wouldn't win. We thought our song was so great."

"What was our song?" Jen looks over when Becca asks this.

"I don't know," she responds. "You're supposed to be the one who knows all the words."

This is usually the point when their mother would turn around from the front seat. They manage to agree on spending the first night in a Dutch efficiency hotel in Salisbury, but it's cold and damp and they can't get any reception on the TV. They miss L.A. They are no longer East Coast girls. "Rudy and Mamie are probably meowing themselves to sleep right now."

"Rudy, Mamie, and Alex."

"Maybe we should have sent Alex over to my place to sleep."

"Let's call him and wake him up!"

After staying up late on the phone to Alex, they drive straight through to Dorset the next day, and stay with Gabby in the production's rented Victorian house. Their room is in a rickety attic, with an old musty gable and a view of an abandoned garden below.

They spend their days wandering around the English countryside, talking about their "grounds," pretending they are in a Jane Austen novel. At night they go to the set, which is in another old house down the road. After shooting ends, everyone gets drunk on whiskey, and makeup artists and grips kiss in the corners. Jen and Becca sit down with Gabby and join the nightly poker game. By the end of their third night, they are both talking to a bald, nebishy lighting guy, the same one they cornered at Alex's promotion party last year. Becca calls him the pheromones man. There is no other explanation for why she and her sister have ended more than one evening glued to this guy. It must be some chemical that mixes with their family's scheme.

On their last day, driving back to London, they stop in a gift shop in a stony old town. Jen discovers an eerie black cross with a jewel-blue overlay that looks as if it was carved from molten rock. She holds it up to show Becca. "Oh, God," Becca says from across the shop. "I saw that at Fred Segal's last week! They were seventy-five dollars." Fred Segal's is the chic department store on Melrose in L.A.. Becca is a regular.

Jen converts to pounds. "Five dollars and they're ours."

They board the plane wearing their black molten-rock crosses, giggling. American suckers.

"You look like Elizabeth Hurley," Jen says to Becca.

"You look like Buffy the Vampire Slayer on her way to her first communion."

"I am a little uncomfortable with it," Jen says. "But it makes me feel as if I have my own club. Now I'm united in sin with my fellow Catholics."

"And the Fred Segal suckers."

Anna

IN A GREEN sheet-cape, carrying a tiny battery-powered fan, Anna is celebrating Halloween as El Niño. The tropical ocean warming is setting off biblical swings in the world's weather, unleashing meteorological havoc on California.

She spent the last two days trying to come up with an outfit for this party Spencer invited her to. Several people in her office, including Ted, are planning to attend. "The problem with working in advertising is that there's a lot of pressure to come up with a good concept. You can't leave the house as a ghost."

She stops by Lizzie's apartment on the way to the party to help her get ready. Lizzie has chosen a shiny pink prom dress, cut off at the thighs, a big bow in her hair, and a button that says "Little Miss Denver." She is going as JonBenet Ramsey. "You are so sick!" Anna says, curling her hair.

Spencer is at the party when they arrive. He comes over and pecks Anna on the cheek. "What are you guys?" he asks.

"You're going to have to guess," Anna responds. He looks at them both, puzzled. Two guys interrupt them with hands in the air. "Spencer is back!" they are yelling.

Anna finds Ness and John in the kitchen, dressed as Prince Charles and Camilla Parker Bowles. Ness has a scarlet A on her chest and a disposable paparazzi camera around her neck. A man in a curvy-arrow shirt is standing next to them. "And what are you?" Anna asks the strange man, popping candy corns into her mouth.

"I'm Rodeo Man," he says. "I'm from New York, so this shirt is costume enough for me."

"New York?" Anna says. "That's one of my previous lives. How long have you been out here?"

"I just moved here last year to start up a CD-ROM company with a friend."

"Your name wouldn't happen to be Ken?" Anna says, looking at him sideways.

"As a matter of fact . . ."

"I used to work with Susan Cassidy," she tells him, nodding. Susan was Anna's old boss in New York, and she used to talk about fixing Anna up with her husband's partner, Ken. Anna can't remember what her boss said about him, but she is impressed.

"You must be Anna!"

"That would be me," she says.

"Oh, God. You're a sticky on my computer."

"That's so . . . flattering." Anna is actually flattered.

"No, no. I would have thrown it away if it meant nothing. I've wanted to call you. We should get together sometime."

They make a date for the following weekend, and Anna excuses herself to go find Lizzie. She finds her talking to Jesus. Anna stares at the costumed man, trying to figure out if his hair is real. Jon-Benet and Jesus, she thinks. Only in San Francisco.

Spencer approaches them with his two friends. "Hey, I'd like you to meet some people who are in from out of town," he says, introducing two tall, clean-cut men. They both have *Preppy Handbook* hair, the kind that hasn't moved in twenty years. They went to college with Spencer. "We're off to the Up and Down club. Can you make it?" he asks Anna.

Anna purses her lips. "Maybe." As they leave, she turns back and watches Ken across the room.

"We *are going* to the Up and Down club," Lizzie informs her a moment later. "Why do you act so uninterested in Spencer?"

"Lizzie, the guy disappeared without word for over a month. I am uninterested."

An hour later, plans solidify as Lizzie learns that Ted is meeting Spencer at the club, too.

"I thought you wouldn't show," Spencer says when he sees Anna. His Halloween outfit, which she hardly noticed at the party, consists of his everyday uniform—worn khakis, a Brooks Brothers shirt, too-thin loafers. He is a sexless dresser, Anna decides. Derek dresses for sex. Distress is very sexy.

"I thought I wouldn't either. Lizzie wanted to see Ted."

"Let's get out of here. I'm dying on the vine," Spencer says.

"Actually, I think I need to go home and get some sleep."

"Sleep? That's not what I had in mind." He is staring over at her, trying to read her. "What happened to you? You used to be so much fun. What happened to that straight-shooter?"

"What do you mean?"

"How come you're not a trash-talking straight-shooter anymore?"

"I'm still talking trash with the best of them. I think we just lost momentum here." Anna feels tired, nothing else.

"Hey, I'm sorry about that. I've been living out of a suitcase since August. I haven't been talking to anyone."

On the ride to his apartment, Anna tries to summon her trash-talk vocabulary. Nothing. It must be squashed under the weight of her forced-indifference lexicon. Instead she is trying to figure out why she is in this cab with him. "I'm sitting there thinking, Why am I doing this again? Oh, yeah, because I'm afraid I'm going to have to say I've gone three months without actually having sex. Then I'll start feeling sorry for myself. It always makes sense when I do the math."

November

The Rules on the Job: Never Call Your Boss and Rarely Return His Calls. If you call your boss, he will immediately know that you like his workplace and he will no longer have to make an effort to make you happy there.

Rules Girls: Joan of Arc. Her hair was a little short, yes, but unlike other saints, she did wait for God to make the first move. Juliet. Makes Romeo think she's dead. Talk about unavailable!

—New York *Daily News*

Jen

JEN RETURNS FROM England to find ten messages on her machine. Half of them turn out to be updates on job prospects. Emily tells her that a job is opening in January at another studio, and Jen is considered the shoo-in. She should expect a call in December. This is a job Jen can get excited about; she can stop making lists. She takes Becca and Alex out to celebrate.

The next day she heads out to meet Dean, the striking, married lawyer, at IHOP. After she saw him at Kate's party, he called to offer help with the job search, and she wants to tell him her good news. Or, rather, she wants to use the pretext of her "good news" to see him again. She thought about him a lot when she was in England, probably because her sister told her not to. In fact, she'd made a list in her head of funny stories to tell him when she got back.

They both order the grand slam. Jen is hung over. Dean is in a bad mood. He is yakking on and on about lawyers and agents and assholes. He doesn't seem too interested in her trip. She is starting to feel like his audience for the day.

"Are you still buff?" he says, picking up on this. "Let me see your arms." Jen holds out her arms, tanned and taut. Then she starts nervously talking about the men she met in England. "I had a fling with this lighting guy," she sniffs. Sniffing is her nervous lying tic. (The pheromones man never even got a peck on the cheek. So much for chemistry.)

"You have the most interesting assortment of men," he says, staring past her. Last time they spoke, she told him that she was seeing Nate and a twenty-four-year-old *GQ* model in New York. So she exaggerated a little.

He quickly changes the subject to a rafting trip he is planning with a couple of friends. They've rented a cabin in Oregon. "I'll come build a fire and make the hot toddies," Jen offers. "I'm afraid of fast water."

"So is Susan," Dean says shoveling hash browns into his mouth. He stops chewing for a second. He has just broken his marital silence.

"Um," Jen says, "you should all go to Colorado. I hear it's great rafting there."

This is too depressing. On the drive home, she decides to call Nate to distract herself. She starts telling him the stories she loaded up for Dean, but Nate is not listening either. "Are you there?" she finally says.

"Yeah," he answers, barely. She is worried that he has slumped back into his depression. Then he starts to giggle.

"What's so funny?"

"Pamela's sunglasses. I'm watching the sex video," he says, chuckling into the phone. The sex video is Pamela Anderson and Tommy Lee's home movie that was distributed around the world.

"Where are you?"

"Sitting in my boss's . . . holy shit."

Sex videos are expensed to the company in Hollywood, especially when they involve high-quotient celebrities. Jen is jealous that she is not in on this, the latest office entertainment. She would have been one of the first people to see the video at her old job. She gives up on Nate and decides to fly home early for Thanksgiving.

JEN IS LEARNING to make the most of her free life; not everyone can avoid the Thanksgiving travel melee. Her parents are thrilled to see her. This will be the longest visit they've had together since she lived at home ten years ago. She spends the first day with her mom, telling her stories about starlets and mini-moguls. Her mom fills her in on her cousins and her seventh-grade locker mate's kids.

By the third day, she and her mother have settled into a routine. They have cereal for breakfast. They read the paper together. They watch *The View.* Then they drive into town and run errands. "This is so much fun," Jen says when they stop at the bakery near her old school.

On the fourth day, Jen makes her mother drive by Billy Bernard's house. Billy was her junior high school crush and this sets off a whole discussion about Jen's stark love life.

"I think you need to find a man who knows how to dance. Someone romantic, old-world," her mother tells her.

"A man with older sisters," Jen tells her, thinking about the baby brother.

"What happened to the date you went on with that man from New York?"

"Date? Oh, you mean Nate? It was really fun. I stayed at the party and he left," she laughs. Every now and then she tries to lie to her parents about her love life, just to make them feel better. Really, she is just upgrading. She did go to a party with Nate. And she and Nate have kissed. Together those two things add up to a date. The problem is that she knows her mother can always fact-check her stories with her sister.

She wakes up the day before Thanksgiving and calls L.A. to check her messages. She vowed she would wait a week, but she can't stop herself. There is a call from a small production company that wants to bring her in for a couple of weeks, one week of which will be in New York. She carves the number into a napkin and takes a deep breath.

She barely touches her cereal the next morning. And she is too restless to read the paper. When her mother suggests they go Christmas-tree shopping the next day, she snaps. "*Mom.* I have to go into the city and find the trades."

"My God," her mother says. "We can't let your father retire. He is going to have to work so you don't have to. Look at you—you have no nails!"

Casey

IT'S BEEN A week since her night with Fletcher, and Casey is on her way to meet Andrew the reporter. She hasn't seen him since the Natalie Merchant concert two months ago. He called to tell her that he's back in town for a while and did she want to come over to watch the Mount Everest movie on TV.

This is a big step. It's an apartment date, and suddenly she's not quite sure she is ready. She's still recoiling from her night with Fletcher and his comment about "bitches," and she's not sure if she can be in some strange guy's apartment right now. Still, she has it in her head that Andrew is the real thing, the one she gets lost in, and she doesn't want him to think she is not interested.

Andrew lives in a walk-up on the Upper West Side, a duplex with brick walls and black-and-white photographs he has taken himself. His apartment is neat. "He has a house cleaner," Casey explains. "I think men get neat in their thirties. It's a good sign. If I went out with someone who had a place that looked like mine, I'd be worried."

They order in pizza and watch the Everest movie in silence. When it's over, Casey finishes her beer and clears her throat.

"I hardly ever hear from you these days," she says, boldly looking him in the eye.

"Don't even tell me you're a *Rules* girl," he says, laughing. "You could have called me, you know."

"Well, I just sort of pegged you for a conservative guy," she says, suddenly turning coy.

With this they begin fooling around for the first time. He is trying to prove that he is not a conservative guy, she is trying to prove she is not a *Rules* girl, and there has been a three-month buildup. Casey starts to get light-headed. This man has been making appearances in her daydreams. There's just one problem—she's afraid she really likes him. It's hard to sleep with someone you really like.

They cut things off before they get too steamy, and he offers to walk her out and hail her a cab. Standing on the curb in his socks, he holds her face with both of his hands and carefully kisses her good-bye.

Casey sends him a one-line E-mail the next day thanking him for dinner. She is breaking the Rules. Rules are for people who can like each other only through manipulation, she tells herself. There is something pure and visceral between them that cannot be disciplined with rules.

She spends the day trying not to tell everyone she knows about him, about how he kissed her, about how she got light-headed. She sets goals for herself on yellow stickies: Don't check E-mail again until after three P.M. meeting. Don't call Maggie. By the time Tuesday morning comes and he has not responded, Casey's friends are hearing about it.

"He's probably on deadline," Maggie says calmly. "He hasn't even checked his E-mail yet."

"Casey, it's that two-day rule," her boss says, clearly not grasping the "pure and visceral" part. "He'll call tomorrow."

"He set you up!" Beth says, her arms crossed into a shield over her chest. "What-an-asshole."

By the time Wednesday comes, Casey feels as if the blood has been drained out of her. No E-mail. No voice mail. "I am in an angry depression at this point. I don't understand it. I thought we were having breakthroughs here. I'm ready to spit, I'm so venomous."

She needs a buoy plan for Thursday night to distract herself, and so she decides to call Randy the ginseng supplier, Oliver's friend. The guy has left her two messages, but she suspected he wanted concert tickets or something and she didn't bother to call him back. Now she doesn't care what he wants. She calls his cell phone and curtly asks if he can meet her for dinner the following night. Before she leaves work for their date the next day, she finally gets an E-mail back from Andrew. "Sorry. I was working. Call me.

Would love to get together." Too late. Their relationship is no longer pure, and the only thing visceral is Casey's venomous determination to forget him.

She tells Randy she'll meet him at a SoHo restaurant near her friend Sandy's house. Sandy has just had her second baby, and Casey plans to visit her after dinner. She needs to spend some time with drooling innocence, uncorrupted life. She calls Oliver in Utah before she leaves work.

"Why am I going out with your friend again?" She's wondering if he's an aspiring musician.

"He just wants to meet you."

"Is it a blind date?"

"Well, yeah."

"That's just great, Oliver. I basically threw myself out the door this morning. I am not dressed for a date."

Oliver lives in Utah. He explains to Casey that SoHo dress codes are not ranking high in his day planner.

The only man sitting alone at the Café Noir is a short-haired ski-instructor type with deep-set dark-blue eyes. His name is Randy. Casey drops her head when he tells her this. "I would love to see a videotape of myself," she laughs when she recounts the tale. "I went in there with my hand on my hip, you know, 'What do you *want?*' And I see this man and this bottle of wine. I think I melted onto the floor."

This was just at first glance. The man actually does ski, he loves sushi, he goes to an acupuncturist, he loves the band Radiohead, he worked on Wall Street, and he gave it up to run a ginseng company. She tries not to laugh. She starts to suspect that Oliver fed him her list, except that she didn't know until now that she had this list. She is waiting for him to reveal himself. When they are finished with their bottle of wine, he mentions his ex-wife. Actually, it's his second ex-wife. The tragic flaws. Everyone's allowed . . . two. What's a couple of certificates? He calls the next day to tell her he had a great time.

*   *   *

A WEEK LATER Casey has had three dates with Randy and one voice mail message from Andrew. She decides to call Andrew back the day after she gets his call, at nine in the morning, before he gets to work. She leaves a message telling him she's going out of town for a while on a work assignment. She still can't bring herself not to return people's calls, even if they are people who don't return hers.

Meanwhile, Randy has invited her back to his apartment for the first time. He has a Central Park West bachelor pad with Persian rugs and antique humidors and silver cigar cutters. He's fancy, a fancy bachelor who's into alternative medicine. He lifts her up and carries her into his room and lays her down on the bed. Then he tells her he's not ready to sleep with her.

"He's got this whole sex thing very under control," Casey reports after the third week. "I'm about ready to burst." By the fourth week, she can hardly think about anything else. They go back to his apartment and he gives her a book on tantra. She knows a little bit about tantra from her yoga classes; it's all about relationships and sex taking you to new heights of "enlightenment." He asks her to read the book so they can talk about it. "I've never met a guy who was interested in this."

She takes the book home and stays up until two in the morning reading it. There are entire chapters about the exchange of energy between men and women during orgasm. "The sensation rises up the spine, lighting up all the energy centers in the body," she explains. "It can change you."

How hard would it be to meet a guy who is interested in this?

Anna

ANNA HAS JUST booked her flight to New York. In three weeks, her divorce will be final. She has been separated from Greg for two and a half years now, and they have been letting the divorce process lag. But the lawyers finally got them a court date, and Anna has chosen to be her own witness for the final day. She doesn't want to spend the extra six hundred dollars just to have her attorney sign papers about her personal life in a faraway courtroom. Instead she spends the money on a trip to New York. "I decided I was going to go and sit there and have some resolution in my life."

Divorce has been a big topic in the news lately. The United States boasts the world's highest divorce rates, and according to *Time* magazine, more wives than husbands are seeking the splits. In an effort to lower the rates, states are proposing laws that require premarital counseling and make divorces harder to get. It's enough to make people just want to forget the whole contractual deal.

Which brings us to Ethan. He left a long message on Anna's machine yesterday. He's back from Italy for a little while, but he is going back to help Sophia have the baby. They still haven't figured out whether they're going to stay together, he said. Then he asked Anna if she wanted to join him on his ski trip in two weeks, "just as friends." Anna played his message for Lizzie. "I thought you explained the friend concept to him," Lizzie said.

Spencer has disappeared again. She hears through Ted that his mother is sick, so now she can't even be mad at him.

And Derek has left to visit his girlfriend in Wisconsin. He was sending E-mails every day, and then he just stopped. She wonders if maybe he's moved already.

After running through this list, Anna decides to call the psychologist and set up another appointment before she leaves for New York City. She needs to be reminded why she left her husband. She needs to be reminded that she was not happily married, that a committed relationship, in and of itself, was not the answer.

"Can we sit little Anna down in that chair?" the therapist asks, pointing to a small empty rocker after Anna fills her in on the latest. Anna nods reluctantly. "Now, look at little Anna and tell me: Would you let this man Spencer spend time with her?"

"No," Anna says squishing up her face. "She's so happy and sweet and she's saying funny things and I don't want him to squash that. He doesn't laugh at her jokes."

"Now, would you let her bother with this man from Texas?"

She pauses for a moment and looks out a window. "No. He's a dreamer. He'll give her all these unrealistic expectations and she'll just spend her life being disappointed all the time."

"Would you let little Anna put up with grief in her job?"

"No." she says. This is why she pays this woman, for coming up with words like "grief" to describe her job. "They'll stomp all over her self-esteem," she says, fully surrendering to the therapy.

On her way home from her session, she decides that she should just never let little Anna grow up.

When she gets back to her apartment, she calls Ken the CD-ROM guy she met on Halloween to see if he can meet for dinner. She would let little Anna go out for dinner with this nice, warm entrepreneurial man. A month has passed since they met, and they have each had to cancel a date. This time, Ken has a cold, but he doesn't want to postpone again. He shows up the following night sniffling.

They swap funny stories about their jobs, the people they both know, San Francisco stereotypes. He tells her about his neurotic family, growing up in New York, starting his own company. When their dinner is finished, he kisses Anna on her shoulder so that she doesn't catch his cold. "Stay away from that arm," he says through his stuffed nose.

"He has the greatest sense of humor," she calls to report after her date. "It's like Monty Python crossed with Jerry Seinfeld. And he laughs at my jokes." He also gets points for starting his own company. "He's a self-made guy. He could take care of someone, but he's still needy enough." And, perhaps, most important in San Francisco: "He's really straight. But he's gay in his appreciation for the details. I think that's a New York thing."

A week later, on their second date, Ken explains to Anna that for the last two years he has had a serious girlfriend who lives in New York. They took a trip to Europe together two months ago, and by the time they got back they decided it was over. This was why he didn't call her earlier.

She's not sure what to make of this. It could just be honesty, the revelation part, or it could be another disclaimer. She shuffles off quickly to avoid the good-bye kiss. She takes the long way back to her apartment, pulling out her Walkman to listen to her Mamas and Papas tape. She never knew the whole time she was married how complicated it could be on the other side. No one had serious ex-girlfriends in college.

Back in her apartment, Anna calls Derek. He left a message the other day saying he was back from Wisconsin and was confused. She didn't think that either little or big Anna could handle him then, so she didn't call him back. But now she is thinking that she owes it to him. She has been confused for several years now, after all.

They make a plan to meet in North Beach, and she finds him standing on a corner, staring down at the sidewalk, one hand on the back of his head. They walk up Vallejo Street, peering into windows, looking for a place to stop. He is chain-smoking and talking about how they shouldn't get together again, how it was just something they had to do once. Then he stops her on the sidewalk and kisses her. A group of people across the street stop and clap. "Isn't she beautiful?" Derek says, presenting Anna to the clapping strangers. She is trying not to grin. If only they knew.

She tells Derek that she has to get up early and hails a cab. An hour later, he calls her apartment, drunk, and wakes her up. "What is going o-o-on?" he says, exhaling smoke into her ear. They talk for an hour about their childhoods and about when he used to adjust her bulletin boards. She has a little trouble getting him off the phone. "Derek," she finally says after a long silence, "I have to go to New York tomorrow and get a divorce. You have to go to Wisconsin in a month and . . . get married. This was not meant to be."

THERE ARE OVER forty people in the downtown Manhattan courtroom where Anna and her husband are finalizing their divorce. Most of them are lawyers. The other couples look like teenagers. Very few people who can afford lawyers actually go to the courthouse.

Anna had over two years to prepare for the day, and through it all, she and her ex-husband have managed to stay friends. This is proof, she now says, that there was never any real charge between them. They have fought over things like credit card debt and who lost interest in sex first, but they have tried not to damage each other. Anna was also the one who left the relationship first. So she didn't expect to cry.

"It was the preamble that got me all weepy. You sit there for hours, everyone checking everyone else out, trying not to look at their spouses. I was looking around and thinking, oh, God, we all failed. I cried off all my makeup."

Anna and Greg sit next to each other in a pew and fidget—like a brother and a sister at church. At one point, he reaches into his pocket and gives her a wool mitten to wipe her face. When their names are finally called, they stand up and approach a podium with a microphone. They had agreed beforehand that she would do the talking; she has been trained to speak in front of clients.

"I just assumed we would say 'I don't,' like at a wedding. They want more details than at a wedding."

In order to get a divorce in New York, you have to sue under one of four categories. Since Anna was the one who wanted out first, her lawyer encouraged her to sue for "emotional distress"—the most common grounds for divorce. She had to write down seven incidences of this distress, including the fight they had in front her family, his refusal to have kids even when they made enough money, the months that passed when he wasn't interested in sex. This was all documented and presented at their preliminary hearing. But in the courtroom, the judge asked Anna to explain her grounds for divorce out loud. "Emotional distress," she said into the microphone, her voice breaking. The judge asked her to elaborate, and she panicked. She looked down at Greg, then announced to the judge and the room that she and her husband "no longer had physical relations." She didn't learn this in client-presentation training.

After they sign all the papers, Anna and Greg stop for a beer in SoHo and try to blunt the tension. They've had plenty of time to accept their list of distresses, and they've settled what was left of their combined debt. Instead, they both try to focus on the future, and Greg asks Anna what she wants to happen next. "I told him that I wanted a more well-rounded life, work, and romance and kids. 'Me too,' he said. Then he paused and clarified that '*eventually*,' he wants kids."

"Then we ordered another round, and I was thinking, what a shame. We want the same things."

BACK AT HER desk the following week, Anna calls Lizzie to find out what she's missed. Lizzie and Ted have decided not to see each other anymore. They had nothing in common. "Oh, but I love Ted," Anna whines. Then she sighs. At least she has Lizzie back to herself.

She pulls up her new E-mail messages, and her pulse quickens when she sees Ken the CD-ROM man's address. He's tried calling her, he writes, but he keeps getting her machine. His old girlfriend is coming to San Francisco to work on a freelance project, and she is planning to stay with him for two weeks. He probably won't be able to see Anna for a while.

Anna doesn't bother to respond. Instead, she starts planning her trip to Greece again. She wants to go by herself and lie on the deck of a big boat in the Aegean Sea and stay in a cavernous white hut overlooking the ocean. And she doesn't even want to get laid.

But by the end of the day, she catches herself thinking about Spencer again. She really did like Spencer, she suddenly decides. "When I first met him, I thought I would be a very bad girlfriend— especially for him. He's very upright. And he dates extremely preppy women from his *caste*. I need a little bit more freedom in a person.

"But now I'm ready to be a good girlfriend to someone. And here's Spencer. He's thirty-five. He's the poster husband. He's the dad from the Dockers commercial. And he's *loaded*. When he goes on vacation somewhere, you have to look up. I could forgive his whole lineage problem."

She leaves Spencer a message inviting him to a party the following night, but he doesn't call and he doesn't show. She doesn't notice until the end of the night, when it's time to go home. "So of course, I've got Lizzie in the corner, and I'm running through this list of reasons why: he met some complete hotty, he thinks I'm not pretty enough, not tall enough."

To make it all worse, their company Christmas party is three weeks away, and after that come the holidays. Anna hates the holidays.

Casey

WHILE ANNA AND Jen are holding the line on uncommitted relationships, Casey is starting to cave. "I don't want to say he's the one," she confesses, now in her fifth week with the ginseng mogul, "but . . . let's just say I'm a better person for having met this one."

Casey and Randy have been spending a lot of time together. He was even thinking of canceling his trip home for Thanksgiving to be with her. She gets sentimental around the holidays, but her parents live in Chicago now, and she doesn't visit them for Thanksgiving anymore. She's spent too many Thanksgivings stuck in a cab on the Queens Expressway, missing flights. So for the last four years she's been sharing a potluck dinner with a few "orphan" friends who stay in the city, and this year she invited Randy to come along. His mom cried when he told her he was thinking of staying in the city, so he booked a flight home.

Before she leaves for her orphan dinner on Thanksgiving Day, Casey gets a call from Dave, the sailing instructor from Labor Day weekend who left for Memphis in September. He's back for the holiday and wants to know if she'd like to join him and his family for dinner in three hours. "Can you believe this guy? Is that classic? I'm trying not to crack up. I thanked him and was surprisingly nice. Then I told him I was late for my Thanksgiving dinner."

On the Sunday after the holiday, Randy calls from Denver to fill

her in on his arrival time. They spend the next three nights together. On the fourth night, she asks him to come with her to her
yoga class. "This is big," she says in her serious voice, calling from
work one day. "I want to do this with him. It's something that's
important to me and I want to know that he's open-minded enough
to come with me. And it's not as if I'm dragging him to aerobics."
After some nudging, he agrees to go with her the following day.
They sit on their yoga mats with eyes closed, and both drift off
somewhere, far away from each other.

A few days later, Casey puts the relationship with Randy to another test. It's been over a month since she saw Andrew the probing
reporter, and he's just left another message on her machine. She
decides that she is ready to see him. "I need to know I overdid that
one."

She meets him for a drink in her neighborhood, and they spend
the first half-hour carefully dodging the question "What happened?" She asks him about his assignments. He tells her about
his trips to Argentina and Peru. He asks her about the years she
spent in Europe. She tells him that moving a lot made her more
curious, more adventurous.

"What happened with the guy you went to the Maldives with?"
he asks, abruptly changing tack.

"Oh, that's over," she says, shaking her head.

He looks at her suspiciously. "You still have feelings for him. I
know you do."

"No, I really don't," she says. She doesn't bother to tell him about
Randy. But she has made up her mind: Randy is the chart-topper
now. "He hit the playlist at number one with a bullet," she announced last week, anointing him the romantic equivalent of the
Spice Girls. Randy is just more her—half downtown, a quarter
uptown, a little bit of Illinois. And Andrew blew it when he never
returned her E-mail. He forced her to make the list, the list of
reasons not to care, and it's still etched in her mind somewhere.

Still, he always manages to impress her. He's sincere and curious;
he asks questions and actually listens to her answers. She gives him

a hug good-bye. "I didn't even have the urge to kiss him. I just realized that I really don't want to have more than one boyfriend in this town. I don't have enough energy for it."

The truth is, Casey's adventure spirit is in the midst of an existential crisis. She's been reading the book on tantric sex, and she's come to a new conclusion about The Act. "It's just too sacred to waste on people."

Andrew has lost his sacred status.

Jen

JUST AS ANNA was leaving New York to head back to California, Jen was arriving. She, too, headed to SoHo, just missing Anna and her officially ex-husband. Jen was starting her two-week consulting project with the independent production company, and when her new boss asked her where she would like to stay, she chose the SoHo Grand Hotel. It's one of the only hotels downtown, and she wanted to be where all the "young" action is.

She calls Fiona and Lynn and invites them to meet her at the hotel bar for drinks. She has the weekend to herself before she is owned by a new company for ten straight days. "Feel free to invite *people*," she tells Fiona, speaking in code. She pulls on a thin black sweater and pins her hair back in a beaded barrette. Then she goes down to the bar and sits by herself at a small table in front of the hotel's huge plate-glass window, next to a gigantic amber lampshade. She looks over at it for a minute: it is twice the size of her. She is Alice, in Wonderland, one of the things she misses about New York. She likes feeling she'll never outgrow it.

Her friends show up late, one by one. She is talking to Fiona when she spots Fiona's friend Elizabeth with a man and two women through the window. "Oh," Fiona says. She was just about to tell Jen that she invited *people:* Elizabeth and her baby brother, Patrick, are on their way up. Jen searches for a nail to chew.

She throws herself into a conversation with Lynn and sneaks a look at Patrick when he enters the hotel bar. He is wearing a big, dark overcoat, and his hair is shorter. Those beautiful blue eyes!

Jen is afraid to get up from her seat. She hasn't prepared for this. And she doesn't want to have to talk to him in front of his sister. That would be mortifying. Besides, he is engrossed in conversation with two people at the bar.

After everyone arrives, Fiona decides they should all move on to someplace more lively, someplace with movement. Chaos is around the corner, a moody, three-level club where people throw big parties. The six of them parade around the different floors looking for a place to stop. Each floor has a bartender with high-arched brows. Behind the bartenders are signs that say "No Dancing."

Patrick is drunk, and now he's mad. No dancing? "What is this, *Footloose*?" he yells to a severely plucked bartender. People are usually begging Patrick to dance. He is like the Arthur Murray grand champion. The women decide to take over a couch. A waitress with a pout approaches them and tells them they will have to order wine or champagne. They have all just paid seven dollars each for drinks, they protest. She informs them that to sit on the couch, they will have to order wine or champagne. "This place is *chaos*," Patrick yells to the waitress. "I am *order*." Jen tucks her chin against her collarbone. She doesn't like scenes. And this is not the Patrick she remembers. The Patrick she remembers was spinning her and catching her.

The waitress asks them to leave. "Chaos!" Patrick barks at her.

Outside in the cold air, Patrick is yelling. "*Order*. There is no dancing in Chaos." Jen is tugging on her collar. "He's like a colicky child," she whispers to Fiona. She is thinking about heading back to her hotel, but Elizabeth has hailed a cab and Fiona is pulling her toward it. They are not sure where they are going. It turns out that Elizabeth and Fiona asked the cabbie to recommend a place for them, and now he is driving uptown to a place he keeps calling "Cheetah." Soon they are pulling onto a street in the twenties, and white stretch limos are lined up in a row next to them. On the sidewalk is a long line of people in fur coats and leopard prints. Cheetah. They ask the cabbie to try again. They get out at a place called F-Stop, sober and quiet.

Sitting at a table in the back of the club, Jen and Patrick finally talk.

"How do you like your new job?" she asks him.

"It gets better each week," he says. She can't really hear him over the noise. She tells him about her work assignment, then asks him if he's getting jaded yet.

"I'm trying not to," she thinks he said. She is trying to read his lips. She gives up on conversation, and says, "What are you drinking? I'm going to the bar."

"Ginger ale."

"Jack-and-ginger?"

"No, just ginger ale."

Jen goes to the bar and orders two stiff Jack-and-gingers. When she returns, two women are dragging Patrick to a dance floor. He looks back at Jen for a moment, then disappears into the crowded room.

Jen decides to return to the giant mushroom hotel.

Casey

RANDY HAS BEEN away again, on business, for a week. The timing is good because Casey has to work late every night to finish her part of a year-end report, and as things heated up between them, they were up to an every-other-night schedule. He calls each night from Boulder to talk about his day. "I've got a big night planned for us," he tells her the Thursday before he gets back.

She leaves work early Friday and walks down to lower Fifth Avenue to look for something to wear. She is jittery with adrenaline. She has just finished her report, and now she has a *planned* big date with a man she wants to sleep with *and* talk to. Plus, she has a reason to get dressed up. She ends up buying a long tulle dress, the kind she could never wear to a work event. She swings her shopping bag as she walks down to the Village to her yoga class. After class, she goes home and takes a nap. "I can tell I'm falling for this guy because all I want to do is sleep and daydream."

He finally calls at six, with a question. "So, where would you like to go to dinner?"

Casey deflates. "Oh. I thought you had something planned."

"I do. I'm taking you someplace nice."

"Well, it's Friday night. We'll probably need a reservation to go someplace nice."

"Nonsense," he says, and tells her to meet him at an expensive sushi restaurant in the Village. Casey arrives early in her new dress and tall boots. Randy shows up in khakis and a pullover. The hostess tells them there is a forty-minute wait.

"First of all," she calls to report later, "I'm all dressed up for our big date, and he's wearing a sweater. Every other night he's dressed up in unbelievable threads. But on a Friday night, the night of the one big date we've planned, he's wearing a sweater.

"He starts telling me this story about his friend in Australia, and I've already heard it. It's been six weeks, and he's telling repeat stories. I tell him I just want the little sushi and he orders the seventy-five-dollar sushi — in Japanese. Complete showoff. Then, halfway into dinner, he tells me a story about getting really drunk at a bar and pinching a girl on the ass. I went crazy. Why are you telling me this? If you did that to me I would throw this sakè on you.

"I thought I was going to walk out on him. He's on some kind of trip, and I'm not liking it. He gets all upset and tries to undo it. 'Let's talk about this. We're not leaving this restaurant until we resolve this.' I finally calm down and recover from it all.

"I stay with him Saturday night. We finally have sex, but it's just not . . . there. He wants me to give him a whole inventory and checklist. I hate that. I'm like, fucking figure it out." But what about that tantric sex book? "I don't think he actually read it. Or maybe he did, and that was the problem," she allows. "He couldn't handle the pressure. You're supposed to focus on your breathing and energy centers, and you're supposed to really concentrate on the kissing." Sounds like work, or Lamaze class. Either way, they didn't make it to any higher planes.

"In the morning, I'm tired and greasy and uncomfortable and things are not going that great. He brings up the ass-pinching thing again. 'You really lost it last night!' he says. I try to explain that it's more about *why* he would feel the need to tell me this, not just that he did it. Then I tell him the dinner thing was over-the-top."

After this, he begs Casey to go to a matinee with him — a soft-lit European romance. He is really trying now. He buys her popcorn and Milk Duds and they scrunch down in their seats. Then he talks through the whole movie.

By herself in a cab riding home to her apartment, she feels herself paling and slipping and she can't figure out why. He checked off so perfectly. Who is going to compete with his list? When is she going to meet another guy who owns a ginseng company and, well, *buys books* about transcendental sex?

December

This [year], it seems more teenagers than ever are going dateless, arriving at the big event with large groups of friends rather than making an entrance on the arm of a boyfriend or girlfriend. "It's the 90s. Everything is different," said Stacey Lee, 18, a student at Jacqueline Kennedy Onassis High School in New York.

—Associated Press

Anna

"EVERYONE'S BRINGING DATES," Lizzie tells Anna, panicked. The company holiday party is a week away, and Lizzie will have to face Ted alone. And because Ted is one of Spencer's friends and will report back, the problem becomes Anna's too. They decide to go alone, together. "Okay," Lizzie says. "But we'll get drunk at my place first."

Anna starts to picture this. What kind of a management supervisor doesn't bring a date to a Christmas party? Her assistant will be bringing her fiancé. She bites a piece of skin off her lower lip, and thinks about calling Ben, her last SSMF (single straight male friend). Last month they got mad at each other over the screenplay they were working on. This might not be a good time to ask him for a favor. Besides, Lizzie has taken to calling him the Discover Card—he's not accepted at too many places. "He's turning thirty-two next year and he still temps," Anna explains. "I can respect getting fired, changing your life. But it just gets to a point where the static sucks the nectar out of you."

She can't call Ben, anyway. Lizzie would kill her.

The next day she gets an E-mail. "I asked Tom from the gym," it says. It's from Lizzie, whose voice she can hear down the hall. "Had to. Don't be mad. We'll get you a date."

Anna dials Ben's number and whines into his answering machine. After several minutes, he picks up. She offers to find him his next temp job if he agrees to be her holiday party date.

At LuLu's, this year's office party venue, Anna spots a man who looks like Derek when she first enters the restaurant. He has matted hair and slit eyes, and she is so happy to see him. Then she realizes that it can't be Derek; he's in Wisconsin. Maybe this guy is a vendor or a new account executive downstairs? Wishful thinking. He is actually the husband of the scariest woman at the agency. She grabs Ben's hand and tours the room.

Lizzie is talking to Ted by the bar. When she sees Anna, she motions to her with a hand gesture that says "save me." Anna drags Ben over to them and does the introductions. Ben gives Ted a coarse straight-man's handshake. He doesn't want to be mistaken for a prop date. In San Francisco, prop dates are usually gay.

"How is the temping going?" Lizzie asks Ben enthusiastically.

"What happened to that new client you were working on?" Anna says, pulling Ted away. She and Ted talk about their clients for several minutes. Then Anna finishes her wine and changes the subject.

"Ted, what is Spencer's *deal?*" she asks, her prop date standing an arm's-length away. "One minute he's E-mailing and calling; the next minute he just disappears."

"Look, I never see the guy. His job is, really, just hell."

Anna tilts her head and twists her mouth to the side. "I know he's been around this month," she says as Ted shifts his weight and sips his drink. "You can be straight with me."

"Well . . ." Ted says carefully. "I just think he doesn't get you, Anna. He went to school in the South, and he's used to very traditional women. I think you intimidate him."

"I am so very *not* intimidating! Ted, do you know what I do all day? I sit in my office and drink diet Coke and bribe the new mailroom guy to bring me *People* magazine. I am very shallow! Do you know what I think about on the bus? My clothes. And not just for one stop. I think about my clothes at every stop!"

In truth, Anna spends her days executing million-dollar national ad campaigns. Sometimes she even sneaks guilty peeks at the *Atlantic Monthly*. But a cultural phenomenon is explained: Who wants to read the *Atlantic Monthly* and be intimidating when she can read *People* and be loved?

Ted tells Anna that Spencer has a friend from Chicago he wants to introduce her to. "He's this out-of-work actor who lives in Chicago now, and all of Spencer's friends just worship the guy. I think he can out-smart-ass you," Ted says. "He's coming to town soon. I'm definitely going to introduce you two and watch the sparks fly."

"That would give me pleasure on so many levels," Anna says later. "One: I'd be in love. Two: Spencer would be seething. Three: pleasure. He would be great in bed and would do something fabulous by then and we'd have this fabulous wedding. Spencer would be an usher and none of my friends would go near him. I'm very busy fulfilling my fantasy."

It took her a day or two before she realized that she was in a good mood again. She wasn't rejected because of how she looked; she was rejected for her personality! "My self-esteem rocketed back," she says with only a hint of irony. "It's not something physical. I knew this all along, I guess. We really didn't *get* each other. And the bottom line with Spencer is, I was always lonelier a few days after seeing him than I was a few days before."

Jen

JEN DOESN'T HAVE an office holiday party to go to this year, and this is making her sad. "You hate office holiday parties," Becca reminds her. "They're awful."

Okay, that's not the only reason she's in a funk. She opened the box, the Patrick box, and now the fantasy is gone. To make things worse, she can't seem to conjure up any images of people or places that will make her feel better.

Becca tries to distract her with the holiday party that she and Alex host every year. She tells Jen they've invited several men for her. After some probing, it turns out they've also invited Dean the lawyer, who just started working on a project with Alex. He is bringing his mystery wife. Just what Jen needs to get into the holiday spirit.

At the party, Jen goes straight for the eggnog, then corners her friend Trish. Becca is trying to pull her sister away and introduce her to the man-spread she has assembled. The first two are watching a football game and barely look up from the TV. The third is on holiday leave from Betty Ford. Her brother-in-law finally steps in and introduces her to the fourth. "Hey," this one grunts. "You like the Packers?"

There is no hope. She spends the rest of the night talking to Trish in the kitchen, pretending to help Becca with the food. "I've always been a lucky person," she says, pouring two more eggnogs. "I used to win prizes at Paragon Park when I was little. I won money in Vegas. I've been really lucky in the jobs I've landed. But I've just never been lucky in love. It's been six years since I've had a serious relationship."

"That's a testament to you," Trish tells her. "You're not a shoehorner. You're not afraid to be alone, so you're not trying to stuff every guy you meet into some role."

"Well, I just feel as though everyone I meet is trying to stuff me into some role. Shrink role. Headhunter role. Fix-my-life-for-me role."

"It just seems that way sometimes. But you're connecting two dots, or maybe six dots, but there are lots of other dots out there," Trish seems to be searching the air for more words of encouragement.

"Just be glad you're not Tom Cruise looking for someone to 'complete' you," Becca interjects, digging into the fridge for more eggnog.

"What's wrong with that?" Jen asks her sister.

"It's so selfish," Becca responds.

"Yeah," Trish says, grateful for the help. "How would you like to be a slice in someone else's pizza?

"It would just be nice to have someone to share a pizza with," Jen says.

Trish sighs. "But you have to go through the pain. Look at Kate. She never would have thought she had any connection with Roger if she hadn't hit rock bottom. You need to go through it before you see things."

Kate enters, smiling, and tells Jen that someone's been asking about her, the groovy guy from her birthday party with the ski hat.

"Guess who he just broke up with?" She whispers a name in her ear.

"Great," Jen says. "Now I'm supposed to follow a porn star."

A few minutes later, Dean comes in and introduces his wife. Jen forces a big smile and brings up the pitch in her voice. "Hi, I'm Jen," she says, but then her smile becomes genuine. Dean's wife is a cute Irish redhead. The most stunning man she knows did not fall for a bosomy starlet! There is hope. Dean looks uncomfortable. He is playing with his tie and gripping his wife's arm. "We're on our way to the food table," he says, excusing himself.

As soon as they leave, Jen and Trish turn to the inevitable topic of every weary L.A. conversation: moving back east. They gripe about the men in L.A. They moan about the claustrophobia of a one-industry town. They're sick of the shallowness, the fact that everyone's in bed by eleven. They have both had this conversation too many times to count. But finally, they get brave enough to actually remember what life in the East was like.

"I always felt I was missing out on something in New York," Trish says. "I don't feel that way here."

"Yeah. You don't get the feeling that people are hooking up here," Jen adds.

"Uh-uh. Everyone is home reading scripts."

"I think the one thing that has kept me from being lonely is that I've never been really involved with anyone here," Jen says. "Sort of self-protective of me, but there has never been any void to fill. Becca thinks I'm too picky, but in a way it's very deliberate. My life is so sane — simple and light. No fights. No traumas. No dread. I've had my share of the heavy stuff. I just don't want any more."

"I know what you mean. But sometimes I think it can be heavy to have only yourself to focus on." The eggnog is starting to take Trish.

Jen shrugs. "I think that's where my cats come in."

Trish nods. "There's a lot to be said for being a pet parent."

So much, in fact, that Jen leaves the party early and drives home to Rudy and Mamie. If she has to hit rock bottom, she is going to be with her cats.

*   *   *

FOR CHRISTMAS, JEN gives her cats the Feline Fantasy—an arched piece of wood with brushes that scratch them when they prance through it. "It's like a kitty car wash," she explains. She plans to sprinkle it with catnip, "kitty pot," to create the perfect feline spa paradise. If she can't be a Hollywood wife, at least her cats can.

Her parents fly in to L.A. on the twenty-third, and they all drive to Joshua Tree National Park on Christmas Eve to take a family hike together. Becca and Alex and Jen are suited up in their California sports gear—Nike hiking boots, Patagonia cargo utility shorts, Armani sunglasses. Their parents are wearing worn tennis shoes and jeans. This was not their idea.

Christmas day is spent at Becca and Alex's new house with Alex's family—everyone except his sister. She is pregnant and didn't come because she can't fly. She has been reading the latest "things not to do when you're pregnant" book, and she is afraid to leave the house.

Jen's mom tells her daughters that having kids today is very different from her day. "Nowadays, people should think long and hard about it. The money, the time commitment, the anxieties are much greater than when I had you two." Then she teases them about being self-involved.

"We are so *not* self-involved!" Jen objects. She and Becca start giggling. ("Do they have day care at the day spa?" Jen jokes later.)

There's another difference for Jen and her sister. Probably because of their parents' encouragement when they were growing up, they have lots of competing options. They can give birth to movies, projects, Feline Fantasy spas. Then her dad pipes up, "My joy in life is my kids!"

"That's because you worked nine to seven," one of the joys of his life, Jen reminds him. "You got the fun end."

"Don't you want to have kids?" he asks.

"I'm not going to have a baby just to have a baby," Jen tells him. "When you make the edict that you must have kids, you set yourself up. Look at how many people can't have kids. Not to mention how many people don't find someone to have kids with. I've always been afraid of people who make five-year plans. My life's too much of a roller coaster. My five-year plan would just mock me."

"Well, if I could do it all over again, I'd make a life plan just to have my two wonderful daughters," her father says emphatically. Jen's mother nods in proud agreement.

The week after Christmas, Jen comes down with the flu. It's the bad kind, the violent kind. The news is full of stories about how all the L.A. hospitals are overflowing with it. Becca and Alex leave soup on her porch and run back to their car. The cats are hiding under the bed. They have never seen anyone puke before.

Curled up on her bathroom floor after the soup comes up, Jen decides the flu is her friend. It has kept her from having to make New Year's plans, and it has taken care of her postholiday diet.

Casey

CASEY DOES HAVE an office holiday party this year, but she couldn't care less about it. She shows up in work clothes and stays for one drink. She sees these people every day, and then again every couple of nights, at functions far more interesting than any office-sponsored party promises to be. Besides, no one is allowed to bring dates to her office party—too expensive—so it's not as if there will be anyone new.

Things with Randy the ginseng mogul unraveled quickly after the pinched-ass story. "That one was a real deflation," Casey says in late December, just over a month after almost crowning him. "He seemed to have been sent. And at first I thought—What is wrong with me? Why can't I like this perfect man?"

After drinks with the probing reporter, she realized that Randy had never asked her anything personal about herself. He talked about himself, fluffed up his feathers, even talked about how much he liked her. But he was never really curious about her. "It just became clear that he wasn't interested in me. Maybe he liked what I did and maybe he liked what I looked like. But it wasn't about me." Then there was the day it hit her—the guy never wore jeans.

"All of the things that checked off, the acupuncture and the ginseng and the tantra, he just did that stuff because it was trendy— like a new business venture. It wasn't him at all. He was about Persian rugs and gilded antiques and Wall Street pompousness— impressing people. I could never have taken him downtown to Ludlow Street to see one of my bands."

Still, Casey continues to believe he was sent. "I think the reason I met him is that he turned me on to that book, the tantric sex book. Now I'll use it with other people."

One reason Casey is able to let go of Randy so easily is that Dave the sailing coach is in town for Christmas. He invited her to lunch, this time with a two-day lead time, and after an awkward hour at a stiff midtown restaurant, he invited her out for dinner the follow-ing week.

"I couldn't bring myself to ask him why he didn't bother to keep in touch for three months. But it was hard for me to turn him down. He's got this low voice and he is . . . just something to look at." As soon as dinner is over, they quickly kiss each other good-bye. Then he calls to ask her if she would like to join him and his brother and sister for their annual sailing trip in the Florida Keys next month. "Oh?" she asks startled. The sailing trip he was plan-ning to take with a "Jane Doe."

She calls to complain: "I don't hear from the guy in three months, and he expects me to just drop everything and spend a week on a boat with him? Where is the logic in this?" She tells him she will think about it and get back to him after Christmas. She is going to spend a week in Chicago with her family. "I need to figure out what I want to do. I feel as if he asked me because he didn't know who else to ask, and because his sister knows me. We haven't even really kissed yet."

✻   ✻   ✻

OVER THE VACATION, Casey surveys each of her family members about the trip. They've heard about her magical Labor Day weekend, then how he disappeared without a trace. But her parents took a cruise ten years ago and they get very excited about the boat. "There is really great rum down there," her sister adds. Her brother pulls out a Crosby, Stills and Nash CD and plays "Love the One You're With." Then Casey has a dream that she's on *Gilligan's Island.* It's unanimous. She is going on another adventure.

The final hurdle is her boss. She calls him from her vacation to ask for another one. Her boss exhales a loud sound into the receiver when she asks for the time off. Then he says he'll have to think about it. An hour later, he calls her back. "You know, when you check off a box on a form, you check off single or married. I remember what it was like to always have to check off single. I think you should take advantage of these things." Okay. Whatever that means. Casey's got the green light. She calls Dave and tells him she'd love to join him.

Casey spends New Year's with her family and her nephew Timothy. She thought about flying back to New York early, but she didn't want to end up frantically running around trying to find somebody to kiss at midnight. "I was sort of holding out to see if someone was going to invite me to a fabulous soiree, but I knew I would have more fun with my family. It's better not to overinflate your expectations for something like New Year's."

She wakes Timothy up just before midnight. He rubs his eyes, then clings to her neck as she dances him around the house.

"Why is everyone wearing birthday hats?" he asks Casey.

"Because it's Timothy's New Year!" she tells him.

"Cake?" he asks her.

"Tomorrow we'll do cake."

The next morning, Casey's brother catches her writing in her journal and starts teasing. "I can just see what you're writing. 'Dave's stock is rising. Andrew is on hold.'"

"Shut up," she says.

Casey is actually writing her resolutions. She wants to focus more on work this year. Her boss is taking a sabbatical in a couple of months, and Casey has been tapped to take over in his absence. This means she will be her own boss for a while, with an assistant, something she has worked toward for ten years. "It's what I've always wanted. I'm going to have autonomy and *help*. It's going to be up to me to make things happen."

Anna

ANNA IS FLYING home to her parents' house in Iowa for the holidays. This will be her third Christmas without Greg, and she has learned to prepare. "I always have a hard time around the holidays," she says the week before she leaves. "They have a way of punctuating loneliness. For nine years, I spent the holidays with Greg." Now she spends the week leading up to Christmas lowering expectations, a sort of pre-dread prep.

The last two years, her family spent Christmas in St. Louis at an aunt's house, so this will be her first holiday at home alone since college. Things are definitely different. She feels weird setting the table, two plates for her parents, two plates for her brother and his wife, one plate for her. And she gets a knot in her stomach when she thinks about calling her childhood friends. People in the Midwest are not as used to divorce, much less young divorce. She's afraid of the nervous looks.

But there are also good things about being home without Greg. She doesn't have to worry about whether he's bored or uncomfortable. At Christmas dinner, she tells funny stories about her dates — the guy who told her she was a sticky, the guy who thought she was a present from one of his friends. Her family gets a big kick out of this. Date stories tend to be much funnier than marriage stories.

After Christmas dinner, the whole family goes to see the movie *Titanic*. Anna cries shamelessly on the drive home. Then she pops in her favorite video, Chevy Chase's *Christmas Vacation,* a family tradition when she still lived at home. Chevy's attempts to light up the house are a nice balance to Leonardo's attempts to live. She falls asleep with Chevy's goofy mug in her head.

On her last night at home, she finally calls Justine, her closest friend from her childhood. The two of them learned to ski together when they were seven. Justine and her husband just had their second baby this year, and she and Anna hardly get a chance to talk anymore.

"Tell me about your job!" Justine says after filling Anna in on her kids. "I get so excited when I see that cereal ad you worked on."

Anna plays down her life to her friends from home. She knows that Justine and her husband struggle with money, and she feels guilty about how lavish her life seems from their viewpoint. She could never talk about the trip to Aspen. "Will Carrie go to Sullivan Elementary?" she asks, changing the subject.

"The thing about people with kids," Anna postulates later, "is that their concerns are bigger. They actually care about what's going on in the planet because it affects their kids. They don't worry about what they'll wear on their next date. They worry about car emissions and the tax base. When you have something more than yourself to think about, you just use more of your brain."

ON THE FLIGHT back to San Francisco, Anna worries about New Year's. She's going out with Lizzie and Jeanne, and they'll probably get decked out; they're still in their twenties. But she just can't imagine putting in the effort. "I'm wearing black pants," she tells Lizzie when she gets home. "My nod to New Year's is that I'm not wearing jeans."

Dressed in a tight black turtleneck and her staple pair of black "cocktail" pants, she meets them at Lizzie's place. Jeanne is making a list of parties they know about, but none of them sound particularly big. They sit down and strategize about the evening's itinerary. They are trying to make sure they will be at the least depressing party at midnight. New Year's can be worse than Valentine's Day when you're single; there is the sense that whatever you are doing when the clock strikes midnight (lingering in the bathroom applying mascara) is what you will be doing all year.

"If we go to the adult party first, there could be four people there, and we might get stuck," Lizzie says.

"We'll just say we're meeting people who are in town visiting, and we have to leave," Anna tells her.

"I say we save the biggest for last," Jeanne insists.

"But everyone will be moving around, trying to find the biggest party to lose themselves in at midnight," Lizzie says.

"Isn't that what we're dong?" Jeanne says.

"Why don't we just stand in the street and greet the passersby," Anna suggests dryly. "That's where all the smokers will be."

San Francisco has just outlawed smoking in all bars and restaurants, effective January first, and Anna is worried that she will no longer meet any distressed men like Derek.

"I've got a beach chair in the closet!" Lizzie says. "We can pull it out onto the street."

They end up getting stuck at a house party hosted by no one they really know. Jeanne found out about it through friends of hers from college. There are women in black velvet cocktail dresses and men in khakis. One of the men turns out to be Jesus, the guy Lizzie met on Halloween. He didn't recognize her at first, without the bow.

Anna looks at her watch. It is 12:15! No one even bothered to pay attention to the countdown. "Why bother to throw a New Year's party if you are not going to bring in the New Year?" she asks Jeanne.

"That's why I wanted to come here," Jeanne says, grinning. "I knew they'd be too cool to bother. The countdown is always the worst part. Too much pressure."

At 12:30, Anna and Jeanne are ready to call it a night, but Lizzie is not. "Excuse me," Anna says, tapping her on the shoulder. "Could you please get your tongue out of Jesus' mouth so we can say good-bye?"

*   *   *

TWO DAYS AFTER New Year's, Anna calls Ben and asks him if he wants to try again on their screenplay. She has some down time with her job, and she misses him.

"I can't tonight. I'm meeting the guys from my basketball team for sushi," he tells her.

"Eew. That's girl food. What kind of basketball team goes out for sushi?"

"What do you mean?"

"It's like dollhouse food. All those accessories."

Ben shows up at Anna's after his dinner, carrying a six-pack of dark beer. They end up watching sitcoms and talking about everyone they both know from college. At ten o'clock, they finally start talking about their screenplay idea.

"Ben," she says, after they realize they still don't have an ending. "Some mornings I wake up and think my life is a horror movie that has no end."

Ben tells Anna that she's suffering from scammer's remorse. They contemplate using this as a title before calling it a night.

January

When men look at the marriage equation, they see a partner who will do the child rearing and housework. Women look at this equation from the perspective of the support staff.

—Jackson Park,

Elle magazine

Casey

JANUARY IS A slow news month. Pamela and Tommy Lee are on the cover of the *New York Post* (they just lost the battle to pull the plug on their sex show). Jerry Seinfeld is on the cover of *Time* (he just announced he's pulling the plug on his no-sex show). At least Miami has the decency to put the pope on the cover of the *Herald* (it's plugging his end-of-month trip to Cuba).

It's Saturday, January 19, and Casey is alone in a hotel in Miami with the *Miami Herald* and Dave the sailor. They've spoken a couple of times since Christmas, but he was back in Memphis, so they didn't see each other. They barely talked on the flight down, and she is surprised when she sees the bed—a giant king-sized one-piece. She thought he might have requested twins, especially since they still haven't really kissed. "I don't know which pillow to take, how far into the middle of the bed I should go."

Luckily, the people next to them are throwing a loud party, and this distracts them from the task at hand. There is gambling in the hotel, and the neighbors are celebrating their winnings. They know this because the walls are made of Sheetrock. Dave leaves the room to go downstairs and complain. He is embarrassed that he chose this hotel, especially since Casey offered to pay for this leg of the trip. While he's downstairs, she falls asleep.

They both act aloof the next day. She can't seem to relax around him. She barely knows him, she realizes, and he disappeared without a word for three months. She has never felt so uncomfortable with someone, and they have a week to go—soon to be joined by his siblings and their spouses. "I was thinking, there is nothing holding me back. This guy is so good-looking, and we're in this beautiful sunny warm place." Except that she feels like a family-picked Japanese bride.

The first night on the boat, the anchor drags, and they have to take turns staying up all night tying knots to make sure they don't crash into the shore. This is a relief. Casey is sharing a small cabin with this guy, and they can barely acknowledge each other. The second night, they sleep next to each other, and nothing happens. She lies awake most of the night, trying not to touch him, trying to remember why she ever agreed to come.

They head to shore the following day and go on a walk along a beach with Margot and Dave's brother-in-law. Dave is telling them all about a dream he had. He was walking along a big open beach in Jamaica with these strange women, and he stepped into this wet quicksand and started sinking. The women wouldn't help him.

When he's finished with this story, everyone is quiet. Casey kicks a shell a little too hard. "It's the biggest cliché I've ever heard," she says later. "He's the biggest cliché I've ever met. I'm supposed to be drowning him in quicksand? *He* invited *me* on this trip. What is this guy so afraid of?" She spends another night lying awake in their cabin, trying not to touch him, trying not to sink.

The next day Margot pulls her aside up on deck and apologizes for her brother. "He's a little scared right now. He knows you're a good family friend, and I think he feels a lot of pressure." Then she explains that Dave was involved with someone seriously for three years and they talked about marriage. He balked. The woman didn't have a life outside of him, and he couldn't handle the responsibility. Then he felt that he had ruined her life. He basically shut down after the breakup.

Casey spends that afternoon sitting alone on the hull of the boat, hanging her feet over the water. She was Dave once. She and Bruce talked about marriage. But then she felt a horrible weight, and she . . . balked. It's just that—she didn't shut down afterward. She broke up with him, and soon she moved on. Women are allowed to end relationships. It's considered an act of courage. When men end relationships, it's considered an act of coldhearted cruelty, the assumption still being that women can't live without them.

Dave is running around the deck in nothing but cutoffs, his crunched stomach turning brown. Still, she can't help thinking—the guy is work. He would be a responsibility too big for her to bear. There is nothing easy about being with him or dealing with him. Of course, she can't stop looking at him in his cutoffs.

That night, they all stay up late drinking sangria and playing cards. Dave has loosened up. He is laughing and telling jokes. He's unburdened himself of his fears. As for Casey, she's already crossed him off the list, so the "perfect man" pressure is off.

Two by two, people leave to go to their cabins, and Casey and Dave are alone on deck. They soon run out of things to talk about, and so they start kissing. A half-hour later, they are back in their cabin. "I was determined to make the vacation fun in some way," she says. "And we did have fun. He was, technically at least, very proficient."

Technically proficient? "It was very much 'raw sex'—you know, not a lot of kissing; lots of panting; then, when it's over, you both collapse on opposite sides of the bed."

It was from opposite sides of the bed that they finally started talking.

"So what's with the quicksand?" she asked him casually, propped up on an arm. "Your sister told me you were just coming out of something."

"Yeah. It's hard ending relationships. It takes a toll. My family thinks I need therapy for commitment problems."

"What do you think?"

"I just think I haven't met anyone who does it for me."

Casey doesn't wait for the "before this." Her chest tightens and she tries to hide a swallow. "Well, I'm glad it's out in the open," she lies.

They have just spent three steamy hours fooling around and he has announced that she doesn't do it for him. Do what? What is *it* for this guy? She seemed to be able to do *that* for him. And they have all these things in common—music, the same movies, his family, balking . . .

Then she remembers the night she looked over at him from his passenger seat. He didn't do *it* for her either. In fact, she felt so empty of any *it* that she cried herself to sleep.

She takes a pillow and a blanket and heads back up to the deck alone. It's a perfect night, clear and still, and she traces the constellations until she finds what she thinks is Cassiopeia. The knot in her chest collapses, and for a moment, just before she falls asleep, she thinks about Andrew.

Anna

HAVING SURVIVED THE holidays, Anna and Lizzie are having lunch in the agency rec room, watching the *Seinfeld* announcement on MSNBC. They both have the January blues. January is a tough month to begin with, but this year is worse: it happens to be when Ethan's baby is due. Anna's been thinking a lot about Ethan lately. Lizzie offers her a tangelo and tries to distract her with a story. "Are you ready for this one?" she asks. "It involves Spencer."

Apparently Spencer and Ted went to the Elbo Room last week and ran into Joanie, the new woman who works in Lizzie's group. Spencer was trying to dance with a tall, nameless brunette all night. The woman disappeared with Joanie at the end of the night, so Spencer made Ted get the woman's number from her at work on Monday.

"So, guess who answers the phone when he calls?" Lizzie asks mischievously.

"Who?"

"Joanie."

"Joanie gave her number to Spencer?"

"No! She *lives* with the woman . . . as in *lovers.*"

"Joanie's gay?"

Lizzie nods. "She pretended she was the woman Spencer wanted to dance with, and she said she would meet him for drinks next week. He's going to go and sit there and just . . . wait."

"You are *kidding* me. Oh, that is so good."

"We should show up and sit next to him and just watch."

Anna laughs, then frowns. Ethan's pregnant girlfriend is a tall brunette. Why couldn't she have been gay?

"This is a freak state, Lizzie," she says, peeling her tangelo. "We have every fruit here, and we have engineered all of them so there are no seeds." She offers Lizzie a tiny wedge. "They need to fix asshole men so they can't reproduce. Seedless assholes."

"What's the latest from Derek?" Lizzie is trying to steer Anna clear of reproduction imagery.

"Oh, he just announced in his last E-mail that he is going to propose to his Wisconsin woman. She grounds him. He couldn't control his life before. I think he thinks he will finally be able to focus on his work life once he can nail down his emotional life."

"What about CD-ROM guy?"

"The ex-girlfriend moved in for good. He says they are still trying to 'figure it all out.' "

"If they couldn't stand each other after two weeks of traveling together, how long will they last living together?" Lizzie asks, trying to offer some glimmer of distraction, if not hope.

As for Spencer, Anna, explains, he seems to be spending a lot more time in San Francisco now that she's over it. They ran into each other at a café last week, and they avoided each other for an hour. Anna was with Ben, and Spencer was with a group of his friends. He finally came over and said hello. That was pretty much all he said. "The guy has never really had that much to say," she complained to Ben. "He's edgeless, round and soft. And he's going bald. But I'm still strangely attracted to him."

Ben shook his head. "If I were Spencer, I would think you weren't very interested in me. I'd think, 'She goes home with me when she wants someone to hook up with, but I can't invest in her.'"

Anna shrugged. "You're right, I guess. But I just want him to say, 'Anna, I really like you.' And then I could say, 'Oh, Spencer, I wish it could work. But it just can't.'"

Jen

"YOU'RE SO HOT."

"You're so big."

Ever since they watched the Pamela and Tommy sex video at Emily's Christmas party, this is how Jen and her sister greet each other.

"Dean said he thought the video was charming, by the way," Becca says.

"When did you see Dean?" Jens says, her voice perking up.

"We ran into him at IHOP yesterday, while you were still sleeping."

"Charming? The only thing charming about it is that they found each other. They're like two developmentally challenged adults. I was watching it thinking, At least there's someone for everyone."

Becca tells Jen she is worried about her. The studio job is on hold, and Jen has stopped looking for other full-time jobs. And she is staying in a lot, watching too much TV, and apparently losing her appreciation for charm. Hollywood charm. She stayed home last Saturday night and watched women's figure skating. Becca puts Alex on the phone to talk to Jen.

"Why don't you come over and plant the garden with Becca?"

"Alex, I piss away my days with her," she tells him. "And she is turning into mom. Last week, she wouldn't talk to me at Kate's house when she saw me smoking. I'm telling you, she looks for things to worry about." Who needs a boyfriend when you have a full-time personal sitter?

Everyone Jen knows has the January back-to-work blues. After a few days of celebrated communal gloominess, she decides that she, jobless, doesn't have to be glum. And she is free to change her daily routine without upsetting some couple equilibrium, so she focuses on her New Year's resolutions.

She wakes up each morning at ten, logs onto her computer, and surfs the news flashes and the Drudge report—evil gossip about people who have jobs and spouses. Then she reads the dailies and the trades—more bad news about people who have jobs and spouses. At two, she wraps a bandana around her head, grabs her sunglasses and a Rice Dream drink, and drives to Runyon Canyon for a hike up to the green ridge. Along the way, she waves to the husky hikers and their pit bulls. She goes home and cooks herself a gourmet dinner from the dusty recipe box her mother sent eight years ago. Then she settles in for *Dawson's Creek.* "I know," she says, "I'm supposed to be watching that *Ally McBeal* show. I'm hooked on a TV show for fifteen-year-olds. I don't know what that says about me."

After two weeks of this—and nudging calls from her mother, her sister, and Trish—Jen decides she needs to interact with people more. One Tuesday, she meets her friend Stewart at an outdoor café on the beach. He is an agent with a flex schedule. He skates in late with a big smile and an announcement. He has a new girlfriend—one of his clients. She's a B-character on a woman's dramedy, and he has been helping her learn her lines.

"I need to get on television," Jen whines. "Even you've resorted to starlets."

Stewart once told Jen she was exotic, something to do with her found-in-nature hair color and breast size. These assets no longer seem to work for her.

"I can't compete . . . got to get me some air time," she mutters. The only way men can get turned on in L.A.: dating a woman who reaches millions of other women.

The next day, after her new morning rituals, she meets up with Nate at the Apple Pan, a burger-and-omelette diner in East L.A.

He's been mad at her because she no longer spends any time with him. She's pulled out of the shrink deal. Got sick of being his crutch all the time. She needs a crutch of her own right now.

"How's your perfect unavailable man?" Nate asks snidely.

"You mean Dean? He's perfect, as always. He calls me every other day with job updates. I think he's taken me on as one of his cases."

"How's his wife?"

Jen scowls. "I'm sure she's fine. I don't ask."

"I can't imagine having a wife," Nate says solemnly.

"That's because you can't picture anyone right now," she says, picturing Dean. "My friend Mark used to say that all his married friends rush home to be with their families, but he rushes out to find a family to rush home to."

"Is that what it's all about?" Nate asks. He had a typical divorced-family upbringing—a couple of stepparents, a couple of custody arrangements. "It's just hard to pursue 'family' in the abstract. When I think of family, I think of Chevy Chase movies."

Jen is different. She has real models. She wants to find what Becca has, what her parents have. "I wish the quest were over now," she tells Nate. "I don't necessarily miss being in a relationship. I don't want to be in a bad relationship. But I can't stop comparing. At twenty-nine, Becca had been married four years. My mom had two kids. I keep wondering, Did I miss something?"

Nate shifts in his seat and changes the subject. He tells her there's a job opening at the TV production company where he works, and she would be perfect for it. Jen just shrugs. She can't imagine committing to one job right now. She still likes thinking she could do anything, everything. If she takes a job, the fantasy will be over. Maybe she will just be an "indie" forever.

She leaves Nate to meet Emily at the Coffee Bean and Tea Leaf. Emily is turning thirty-eight next week. She is one of seven kids, and now it looks as if she won't have any. This is fine with her: she decided several years ago that she has no tolerance for kids. Screaming makes her really anxious. She doesn't even look at babies. And she has a pod of disciplined, adoring nieces and nephews who call her every week. She's the cool aunt they draw fridge pictures for.

"When I was growing up, I never really thought I wanted to have kids," Jen tells her. "But last week, this baby was staring at me over his mother's shoulder at the Third Street Promenade, and I followed them down the street. The mother turned and looked at me like I was a sadist, then she grabbed the kid and ran away. So, I've been thinking, I need to find a good man. A good dad. But that's just not going to happen in this town."

"No way," Emily says, shaking her head. "The men here are way too self-involved—and that means entirely too much work for you."

"It just wouldn't be fun," Jen says.

Mothers are on trial again. A British au pair was accused of shaking a baby to death in Massachusetts last February, and the "nanny trial" has the call-in radio squads blaming the career mom for leaving her kid with the hired help. No one's said a word about the dad.

"This woman I went to college with works with her husband in New York," Jen says, "and they drop their kid off at day care together on their way to work. Meanwhile, she has to get the kid ready alone. Last summer she went to our college reunion and he agreed to take care of the kid for the weekend. On her way out the door, she answers the phone and it's the baby-sitter he's hired to watch the kid on Saturday. He told her that he needed to see his friends. He couldn't go *one day* alone with his one kid!"

"And they demonize women for wanting to work."

"I just don't want to hate my husband because we have a baby. If I have a husband like Alex, I will totally have kids. If I marry a selfish ass, someone who brings out my own selfish ass, I won't have kids."

February

Handsome—With Love's light wings did I o'er-
perch these walls:/For stony limits cannot
hold love out,/And what love can do, that
dares love attempt. —Romeo and Juliet 2:2
Happy Valentine's Day. M

                        —Monica Lewinsky,
                            The Washington Post classifieds

Casey

SO MUCH FOR slow news months. The sex scandal of the century just broke.

It almost seemed as if the year's events were building up to it: pilot Kelly Flinn and the married civilian, Frank Gifford and the stewardess, Paula Jones and the president's "distinguishing characteristics." What could top this? Only a White House intern and an Oval Office blow job.

After the scandal broke, Casey got a call from an old friend from Germany, telling her that the United States, her country, was pathetic. "I know, it's embarrassing," she responded. "I don't want to hear about it," she told her friend.

The hard part, Casey decides, is keeping the crudeness of national events from destroying her Valentine spirit. Every February she makes a couple of homemade cards and sends them out to a few friends and her brother and sister. It used to be her favorite thing to do in art class: "I was very into it. Feathers. Glitter. Purple construction paper." Now she sticks to typing paper and a few photographs and an old box of colored pencils.

Back in her apartment, she tries to hide the homemade cards she has just glue-sticked together. Andrew the inquiring reporter is on his way over for the first time. He called and left a message while she was in the Florida Keys, and it couldn't have been better timed.

He shows up ready to take her to a smoky jazz show at the Village Vanguard. They split a beer as he wanders around her living room, investigating the photographs, pulling books from her shelves. He lingers on her *Yoga Journals*, then moves on to her *Condé Nast*

Travelers. She finds him in the dark of her hallway as they're leaving and kisses him.

After the show, she hints that she wants to go uptown to his apartment, but he doesn't take the bait. "Let's see if your roommate's home," he says instead. She's not. They turn on the TV and open beers, and soon they are draped all over each other. He stops them before the clothes come off. After a few stuttering starts, he tells her that he has a girlfriend. He's not sure where it's going. "It never even dawned on me," Casey says later. "Here I've had four other men in my life and it just never dawned on me that he might have someone other than me."

Andrew explains that he's been shifty because he doesn't feel right about getting involved with her until he figures out what's going on with his other relationship. They decide they need to keep things on hold for a while, until he figures it all out. Then he starts telling her about a scene from *As Good As It Gets*.

"Did you see that movie?" he asks her.

Casey starts nodding but stops herself. "I saw that movie with *you!*" she says, hitting him.

"I know," he laughs. "That was just a test. Something tells me I'm not the only man in your life."

"What do you mean?" she says pulling her knees up to her chin.

"Well, what's up with this sailing trip you just took? Some friend's single brother?"

"We're not dating."

"It's really romantic down there, Casey."

"Well, okay, it was sort of a date."

"A date?"

"A romantic trip. But it really fizzled fast."

What she doesn't tell him is that on the final night of her romantic boat voyage with the perfect man, she thought about him.

CASEY IS IN a cab heading downtown. She is meeting Andrew in Chinatown for dinner. She is feeling really queasy—the jerking of the gas pedal, the smell of the streets, the sudden image of the Valentine's Day card.

Last week, after she finished dropping all her homemade cards into the mailbox, she decided to send one to Andrew. She spent fifteen minutes trying to figure out how to sign it, then left it blank. Then she didn't hear from him for five days, until he called last night to see if she wanted to go get dim sum. The subject of the card did not come up.

Her stomach settles down the second she sees him. But after a half-hour, when he still hasn't mentioned the card, she starts playing with her dumpling. "So, did you receive any valentines?" she finally asks, staring down at her plate.

"Oh. That was from you? Why didn't you sign it?"

"I don't know. I didn't know how to sign it."

They quietly finish their dinner. In the cab on the ride home, he invites her to his apartment. She looks over at him and waits for him to explain.

"I ended things with the woman I was seeing," he says.

She stays over at his apartment for the first time, but things are cautious. She is trying not to scare him, and she is trying not to scare herself. Still, he seems to be climbing his way back up the charts. "He's the single best kisser I'll ever meet. So good I can't even define it. He's just attentive and confident—none of this 'Here, I'm going to slurp your face while I do something else.' He was very focused and very natural."

Still wide-awake at four in the morning, she gets up to go to the bathroom and takes a private tour of the apartment. His place is charming and warm, not too lavish, not too sparse. There is brick and wood and paint and texture; there are photographs with meaning. She stops to count the number of closets. By the time she leaves the next morning, she has figured out a place for her couch.

Five days go by, and she doesn't hear from him again. This time, she is furious. She is running out of excuses for him, running out of friends who will still tell her she is overreacting. He finally calls from Boston and acts as if nothing's wrong. She tries to forgive him.

He is absentminded, she reminds herself. He gets lost in his own world. "I just don't know if I should accept this. On the one hand, he does these rude things. But then when I see him, he's completely attentive."

But, she has to admit, his disappearing acts have kept her interest. "I probably would have felt the gap more if it were all on me. He's very Upper West Side, not a downtown guy. I struggle with my wardrobe, what we are going to do together, the money issue. He talks a lot about wanting to make more money. We're definitely different."

But now her thirty-fourth birthday is approaching, and Casey is getting cranky. She has no set plan to see Andrew again, and it is too soon to rely on him to be her birthday date. She has also had a lot of letdowns this year, so her enthusiasm is waning.

He finally calls her at work just before the weekend. The assistant puts him on hold and asks her if she wants to take the call. They both scrunch up their faces for a few seconds, trying to decide. "What the hell," she says. "Send him in."

Two minutes later, even with the assistant in earshot, Andrew has her laughing out loud.

CASEY DECIDES TO throw her own thirty-fourth birthday party. She waits until her brother Brett comes to town and invites about fifteen friends to meet them at a new bar off Gramercy Park. Her closest friends get there first—Maggie and Beth and Alison. Then people from her old job. A few friends from college. "When are your men arriving?" Beth whispers, handing her a tiny cigar. It turns out Casey has invited both Andrew and Stefan to her gathering. Everyone is waiting for the high moment when they will meet.

"Originally, I had planned to have all of them in the room just to see what would happen," Casey tells Beth. "Stefan, Andrew, Dave, Fletcher, Randy. Then I got scared and narrowed it down to the two I really care about. My only fear is that Andrew will flip out about Stefan. He's really insecure about that trip we took to the Maldives."

Stefan arrives first, and the women all turn at once to look him over. He does have a presence—the presence of a world-weary man. He never did bond with her friends, and only her brother approaches him. Brett met Stefan the last time he visited New York. Casey is about to head over and say hello to Stefan when she sees Andrew come in behind him. She turns and makes a quick trip to the bathroom at the other end of the bar. The idea of these two worlds, two Caseys, standing next to each other is making her woozy. She watches them for a few minutes from her safe distance. Andrew is interviewing all her friends. Stefan is staring up at a TV, talking to Brett.

Just before he makes a fashionably early exit, Brett introduces Stefan to Andrew. They barely register each other, but Andrew looks down at his hand after the odd European finger shake. He has never had his fingers squeezed by a man before. Casey, drunk and distracted by the collision of people, spends the rest of the evening on a couch surrounded by a pile of girlfriends and presents, smoking her little cigar.

Andrew takes Casey out to dinner the following week to celebrate her birthday alone. He talks about his apartment crisis, how his rent is going up and he has to find a new place, and asks her what she thinks about the west nineties. She has never been a west nineties kind of girl. "It's great up there," she tells him.

She spends the night at his apartment, and this time they both let go. He is securing his place at the top of the charts. "He's just a great lover—confident and natural and just right there with me. With Randy and Stefan I always sort of drifted off somewhere, distracted. With him, I'm just there."

The next morning, Casey leaves Andrew's apartment early. It's Saturday, pouring cold rain, and she has to oversee a local news shoot of a heavy-metal band's in-store appearance. She races home to change, shoving her hair up into a black knit hat and adding a pair of amber-tinted sunglasses—the kind fan-embattled rock stars wear. Then she throws on a pair of heavy-heeled brown boots and a puffy black coat. She climbs her way through the screaming teenagers to get inside the Sam Goody store. "Everywhere you look there are these little dirtbag metalheads," she tells her video crew. And now she has to corral them so the cameras can capture their shrieking, worshiping faces.

Her ears are ringing when she calls Andrew from a pay phone on the street a few hours later. He's spent the day looking for apartments, and he wants to stay in and order food. "Come up," he says. "I'd love to see you."

The first thing she notices when he opens the door is his knit sweater vest. She has just spent her day with greasy-haired teenagers in faded black T-shirts. She and Andrew open a bottle of wine and talk about their day. She tells him about the metalheads and the cameramen and the bewildered onlookers. He tells her about taking his nieces to the park. Then he asks Casey if she can imagine having kids in the city. She takes a big sip of her wine, then tries to imagine kids, period.

"Can you imagine having them anytime soon?" he asks her after the wine is gone.

"Yeah, I could," she says after a long pause.

Later, when she replays this, she concedes that it is puzzling: people want to be in relationships only with people who have a life outside of them, but babies don't have any life outside of them. And talk about commitment—eighteen years of utter dependency. If Andrew can't even be in a two-nights-a-week relationship, how does he think he can manage an every-night-for-eighteen-years relationship?

Casey tries to picture how it would work: a nanny comes in during the week; they play with the baby after work from seven to ten; he disappears for two weeks on some reporting assignment; she scrambles to find an overnight nanny when she is sent out of town at the last minute; she's the one who has to go see a shrink when the kid calls the nanny "mommy." They fall asleep on his couch watching TV. Alone in her apartment the following night, she calls her brother. "I suppose I could quit my job," she tells him after recounting her conversation with Andrew. "I could do it. I could live simply. And I have had my fun. I really do like him."

"I can't really picture you not working, Case," her brother says. Then he tells her to try and focus on this one. "You're too all over the place with these guys. Give something a chance."

By the end of the month, Casey calls to report that she is starting to picture things with Andrew, that she can imagine settling down. Does it still bother her that he is not entirely "her"? She had mentioned once that settling down sometimes felt like *settling*.

"Well, I've struggled with this. I have had a whirlwind couple of years and lots of disappointments. And I do believe that you run out of chances. Is Andrew exactly what I pictured? No. Is he exactly me? No. But when I'm with him, I don't question everything. You can spend the rest of your life doing the 'what ifs' — coulda, woulda, shoulda. That's bullshit. That's a terrible way to live. There will be temptations all the time, things that make you question everything. But I'm completely lost in the moment with him, and you can't ask for a better chance than that."

FOUR MORE DAYS go by before Casey hears from Andrew again. She should be used to this by now. She calls her brother again, and this time her voice is edgy. "I just hate feeling like his weekend date. All he has to do is check in with me for a minute. How does he know someone else isn't going to poach me?"

Anna

"I HATE CARD shops," Anna announces one day in early February. She doesn't share Casey's enthusiasm for Valentine's Day. She has just spent her lunch break trying to find an appropriate birthday card for her assistant. "Congratulations-Happy-Happy-Happy. Can you please show me the Brimming with Bitterness section?" The impending holiday is making her a little moody.

She didn't always feel this way. She used to love the days when girls would get paper hearts and printed candies from every boy in the fourth grade. What happened to those boys, she wonders. What happened to all that sentiment?

Luckily, she is spending the week in New York for a "Women in Advertising" conference. There will be a whole ballroom full of women who see Valentine's Day strictly as a marketing opportunity. And with all the panels on glass ceilings and networking and management styles, any wallowing over a Hallmark holiday will just seem girlishly silly.

The other good thing about New York is that all her friends are single, or gay, or gaily single. She makes plans to go out with Henry the night of the fourteenth.

The truth is that, more than any other time of the year, Anna misses Greg around Valentine's Day. February is when they decided to separate, three years ago. For the previous ten years of her life, her biggest fear about February fourteenth was just being able to get a reservation somewhere. "The things I miss about Greg have nothing to do with sex or romance. I miss his friendship." Greg has started seeing someone seriously, and he and Anna no longer really talk.

She spends the first two days of the conference roaming the seminar rooms, looking for old friends from previous jobs, sharing stories about terrorizing clients and torturous campaigns. There are women from London and Milwaukee and Hong Kong. There are people who handle countries and the Red Cross and gigantic breweries. But she spends most of her time talking to the women who still work in New York. They are the people she will be working with when she moves back — at thirty-five. They will be her social network when she has to reconquer the Manhattan frontier. Plenty of her old colleagues in New York are still single, and they don't even seem to notice.

She sneaks out from a "branding" dinner on Wednesday and heads to a dark bar in the West Village to meet Michelle. She has to roam the bar looking for her and finally spots her sitting in a booth, surrounded by a bunch of people she doesn't recognize.

Michelle introduces them as friends from work, and Anna suddenly finds herself squashed in next to a tall man in black-framed glasses. The people on either side of them are deep in conversation, but the tall man is staring straight ahead at nothing. She stares straight ahead too but swivels her eyes to the corner of their sockets to look him over. He's itchy—foot jiggling, fingers drumming, veins popping. "Classic A.D.D. I'm thinking, what a match we'd make: two checked-out people fidgeting."

She turns to the man on the other side of her and asks him what he does. He's an ad executive, living in L.A., visiting New York for a client meeting. He is older, forty-five is her guess, and he has glassy blue eyes and a thick voice. They swap notes about their jobs, her conference, California. "You should look me up," he says before scooting out of the booth. He is late for a meeting with more people. "Get my number from Freddy," he says, pointing to the itchy man sitting next to her.

The tall man, Freddy, finally turns to her and peers out over his glasses. "And what do you do?" she says, tilting her head to match his. He tells her that he has just sold his political advertising business. He looks about twenty-seven, but she plays along. "Mmm. So what kind of clients do you handle?"

"Oh, you know, Ferraro, Feinstein, Figar . . . amo . . ."

Anna nods her head slowly and narrows her eyes. "So how do you feel about the Federal Trade Commission regulations?" she asks. She is up for some good verbal sparring. He seems skilled; he makes up a long-winded answer. She smiles at him. They have an unspoken arrangement to bullshit each other until last call.

After an hour, Anna excuses herself to go to the bathroom, and when she returns, the tall man is gone. In his place is his cute but angry short-haired friend. "Are you wearing thong underwear?" he asks her.

"As a matter of fact I am," she says, without considering whether she should be offended.

"I'll pay you five dollars to see your thong underwear," he says. He looks about fifteen years older than Anthony Michael Hall when he delivered this line in *Sixteen Candles*.

"Okay—there are various reasons why this won't work," Anna responds. "First of all, I can't believe you think I'm only worth five dollars." The twitchy man has slid back in on the other side of her. She looks over at him. "How about if I offered you five dollars to see your underwear?" she asks him.

He pushes his glasses up on his nose. "Only five dollars?"

"Thank you," she says turning back to his friend.

One by one people are leaving, including Michelle. The tall man continues to weave his tall tales. Anna is still nodding. "I was looking at him, thinking—good-looking, stylish, clever, an asshole. This guy is clearly full of himself. If my ego ever gets that big, I want my friends to stage an intervention."

Still, she is attracted to him. They share a cab to the East Side as he tells her about his mother. She is very cool, he explains, possibly his best friend. Then he asks if he can come up to her hotel room and see her thong underwear. A half-hour later, when she reveals that she is wearing the full-coverage kind, he threatens to leave. "The only reason I came up here was to see your thong underwear," he says. He is wearing plaid flannel boxers.

When Anna tells him sex is not an option, he tells her he carries condoms.

"Look," she says, "clearly you respect women—that story about your mom and all—so I'm pretty sure you can respect that I don't want to have sex with you."

Foiled. With the bantering over, they fall asleep.

When she gets ready to leave her hotel room the next morning, he asks if he can stay and sleep in. After she's gone, he orders room service. "I suppose I would have done the same thing," she says when she gets the bill. "When I was twenty-one."

Anna spends Saturday the fourteenth with her friend Henry, as planned. They are going out dancing at a gay club in Chelsea. They spend the day walking around the Village trying on shoes. Anna buys a pair of girl-motorcycle boots to match Henry's, then she drags him into a Banana Republic to buy a low-cut fitted silk T-shirt. "I don't want the boys to think I'm a lesbian," she tells him.

The club is loud and full of men, their faces lit by blue lights.

Anna is the only woman for as far as she can see. There is a sunken-pit dance floor, and half the guys have taken off their shirts already. Some of them look like Canadian hockey players—big backs, choppy haircuts. People are lining the pit to watch them dance to Thelma Houston. It's hot, and Anna and Henry are blotting their foreheads. "Those guys down there have the most well-placed sweat of anyone I've ever seen," she yells to Henry over the music. "How is it that their chests sweat and nothing else?"

Two men yank Anna off the raised platform and into the pit, and suddenly she is squeezed into the center, shiny chests all around her. "It's very kitsch to dance with the girl," she explains. She has done this before. She stares down at the floor and laughs as two men move in on her. Arms go up in the air with Thelma's voice, and everyone screams the refrain. "*Baby* . . . my heart is full-a-love and it's *hot-for-you* . . ." Anna reaches up to pull Henry into the pit, and begs him to hoist her up in the air—like Patrick Swayze in the finale of that Jennifer Grey movie. They both end up collapsed on the floor.

She never knew Valentine's Day could be this much fun.

Jen

JEN IS GETTING ready for a dinner party at Emily's house, slightly panicked because she is going to miss *Buffy the Vampire Slayer,* and Buffy is going to get laid tonight. Jen has become attached to the show, especially to Buffy's boyfriend. Jen's friend Stewart knows an agent who represents one of Buffy's friends—he just designed her a "Friends of Buffy" Web site—and Stewart has promised to send Jen early-release tapes.

One of the great things about being unemployed is that Jen has a lot more time to shop for men—TV-shop, that is. Sometimes she can actually order them up—her very own home Boy Shopping Network—by calling her agent friends, requesting their vitals, and begging for an invitation to their next public event. Or she simply requests the early-release tape. No sense in leaving the house if you don't have to.

Emily lives in Hollywood Hills, a half-hour away, and Jen arrives late. People are scattered all over Emily's house, sitting on the floor, leaning against the tables. Jen doesn't recognize anyone. She feels like the new kid in town all over again.

She sits down on the couch next to Emily. Two men with goatees are on the other side of her, talking about the creative merit of the Pamela and Tommy video. "I thought the Tommy angle on the blow job with Pamela's giant sunglasses coming at it was very Hitchcockian," Jen interjects. The man with the glasses laughs. He looks about thirty, but Emily pulls her aside in the kitchen a half-hour later to explain that he is a *very wealthy producer* in town from New York. The other people with him are part of his *entourage*. He and Jen spend the rest of the night sharing stories about bad movies and Pamela Anderson, and then he asks her if he can take her out Saturday when he's back in L.A. "I'll see you next weekend," she says as she's leaving. Then she realizes that Saturday is Valentine's Day. Yikes.

There are three messages on her machine the next day when she returns from her morning hike. The first one is from Kate. "I can't believe you're going out with Jeff Simms. Eew. He's horrible." Okay. Kate hates all men with money, Jen reminds herself as she deletes Kate's message. She's kind of radical that way.

"Jen, it's Barbara, Emily's friend. Listen, do not get into a sexual relationship with Jeff Simms. He's one of my best friends, but I wouldn't do it." All right. He's probably pulled something on Barbara's friends, Jen explains to herself. She's had to deal with lots of shrapnel, lots of crying people yelling at her.

It's time to call Becca for permission. She's a little leery after hearing about the messages. "The way I see it, any guy I date over thirty is going to have a rap sheet as long as my arm," Jen pleads with her sister. "I can't listen to other people's take anymore. If I do that, I can't date anyone." Then she tells Becca that she is meeting Dean for lunch the next day. Becca okays her date with Jeff Simms.

But then Saturday afternoon comes, and Jen still hasn't heard from Jeff. She's debating whether to start prepping, and so Becca comes over to do the prepping for her. She heads to the bedroom and starts pulling clothes out of the closet. Jen stays out in her living room, still dressed in her mukluks, watching the Clinton-Monica update on TV.

"At the rate I'm going," Jen announces to Becca, "the only decent men who are going to be left for me will be interns. Even Stewart has a serious girlfriend now, and he's only twenty-six. I am going to have to keep lowering the bar."

Jen has never been interested in moguls before. In fact, she's never been interested in anyone over thirty. She's excited about "dating up." "In Hollywood, people don't respect dating down," she explains. "You look like a dope if you date a bimbo—unless it's some actress who can make you a ton of money."

But what about Patrick? He was only an intern when she met him. "Yes, but he wasn't *my* intern," she responds. "And he didn't live here. You don't date the people you work with. Period. That's my problem with this town—one industry. Everyone works with everyone. It can get so ugly." People should be smart enough to know the consequences of dating their intern, she concludes, and if they're not, they shouldn't pretend to be in charge.

Speaking of consequences, she is already paying the price for "dating up." At four o'clock, when Jeff still hasn't called, she picks up the phone and dials Nate's number. She asks him to meet her in two hours for a drink. "Uh, okay," he says, afraid to ask any questions. "Can we go somewhere that has darts?"

Her date finally calls at five-thirty. "Hey, how's it going?" he says from a car phone, over static. "Can you meet me at Barfly in an hour for dinner?"

"I've got plans," she tells him in a clipped voice.

"Look, I'm sorry I called so late. I was with these people all day." *Day?* You had all week.

"That's fine. It's just that I've got plans."

Becca is now standing in the doorway of Jen's bedroom, one hand on her hip. In the receiver, Jen hears Jeff sighing through the static.

"Look, I'll try to meet you later for drinks," she finally says to him.

"I know, it's the appropriate thing to do. Meet up for drinks."

"I don't want to get into a fight with you, but you called me at five-thirty, and now I've got plans."

"But I want to see you. Meet me at Barfly at seven."

Now she's pissed. She tells him she'll meet him at eight. She pulls on a pair of jeans and a white T-shirt and meets Nate at a lounge bar in West Hollywood. When she shows up at Barfly, somewhere closer to nine, her date is at a table surrounded by six people. "He's a people collector," she explains. "An entourage man. He lets you know he's a too-busy guy."

He slides out of the booth to say hello to her and buy her a drink. "So what do you think of Monica's makeover?" he asks her when he gets back.

"I think she got the newscaster special from Nordstrom's," Jen tells him.

He laughs. "Yeah, she does kind of look like *Live at Five*. So who did you use to work with at your old job?" Jen tells him about her former bosses. "Oh, Mike and Jimmy. Good for you." The shortened first-name drop. He's been taking power classes. She worked *for* them, he works *with* them.

"Yeah, it was . . . good for me."

"Hey, did anyone ever tell you you look like the actress on *Chicago Hope*?"

Pretty soon five more people arrive, and they are swallowed up by a party. After an hour talking to a publicist at the end of the table about presidential sexual rights, Jen tells her Valentine that she has to leave.

Anna

ANNA IS MAD at San Francisco. Whenever she is annoyed with her job or her life, she blames the city and plots her escape. She has bumped up her move back to New York. "In a year, if I'm still a professional caffeine pusher," she says. "My bosses will be very nice about me wanting to leave by then. They are sensitive and they want everyone to be happy. That's one of the reasons why this would be a great place to settle down. The people are truly great. But sometimes it seems as if everyone I know is back east."

It's late February, and Henry is in town for the weekend. Everyone back east always wants to visit Anna in San Francisco. She has planned a night out with Henry and Lizzie. San Francisco's nightlife is very mixed—straight and gay go, openly, to the same places. They head to a place south of Market and pull up stools at the bar. Anna stops and says hello to two drag queens on her way to the bathroom. She tells them that she had to say hi because she misses her friend Patrice, a drag queen who lived down the hall from her in Manhattan. "Do you know Patrice?" she asks them. "No," they say flatly.

She heads back to Henry and Lizzie at the bar. "Even the drag queens here don't get me. I was _kidding_. I should have asked them if they knew Mrs. Doubtfire."

Henry and Lizzie have ordered Jack Daniels and ginger ale. They are staring up at a TV, watching a solemn newscaster talk about the presidential sex scandals. "Get over it, world," Anna says to the TV. "These women consented to it. They knew what they were doing. It's not as though anyone is surprised by it."

Most people in San Francisco seem as if they couldn't care less if the president was having sex with his dog, Buddy. But Lizzie is upset about the Monica Lewinsky story. She has been contemplating religion and rules and right and wrong. She needs to know that if she gets married, it is a pact, an understanding that nobody will cheat. She needs to know that a betrayal of trust is not just another Jay Leno joke. "In Lizzieville, there will be such a thing as right and wrong," she tells Anna. "We have to live by some rules if we are going to survive in the world, if we are going to have any kind of lasting human relationships." People can't just act on every impulse because eventually there won't be anything left to them, she concludes.

Anna admires Lizzie, but she has also lived through more. "What happens in Lizzieville when you and your husband fall out of love but you don't want to put the kids through a divorce? Or what happens when you just need a break? Sometimes rules just make it harder to deal with the gray areas." If you decide cheating is evil, what do you do after you've staked your life on someone who cheats? What are you if *you* cheat?

Henry is on Anna's side. He knows about learning to deal with the gray areas. Meanwhile, Anna has spotted a handsome brown-haired man over Henry's shoulder. He is standing in the corner by himself, staring up at the TV screen, too. He falls into one of the gray areas.

"Don't turn around," Anna whispers to Henry and Lizzie. "Beautiful man at eight o'clock." They each take turns gazing casually over at him. Then they place their bets: "Gay," Henry says firmly. "Straight," Lizzie and Anna declare hopefully. "Let's bet a round of Jack Daniel's shots," Henry says. It's a deal.

Anna swivels off her stool and approaches the beautiful man with her hands clasped behind her back. "We were trying to figure out which team you were on," she says smiling up at him.

"I'm with them," he nods over at the drag queens. Anna mugs, then invites him to join them for a shot.

"You didn't get anyone for me," Lizzie whines after Henry and the man start talking. Anna orders a round of Jack Daniel's, then walks up to three men at the other end of the bar. One of them is wearing a flannel shirt, the other two are in untucked oxfords. "Hi, I'm Anna," she says, tilting her head into an apologetic plea. "Listen, my friend is over there by the bar, and she's a little blue and we are trying to find straight men."

"I'm Bob and I'm straight" the tallest one says, holding out his hand. Anna grabs it and pulls him over to the bar.

"Well, are you interested?" she says, presenting him to Lizzie. Lizzie has turned back to the TV. She is pretending she doesn't know Anna. The man lingers for a few seconds until Lizzie turns back around. "Hey," he says sheepishly. Lizzie apologizes for Anna's "behavior." Then they start talking. It turns out he knows Jeanne from the gym. He was her gym orientation trainer. "This city is so small," Lizzie says nervously. She is trying to remember if this is Jeanne's gym crush, if she will get into trouble if she brings him home someday.

Having paired up her two dates, Anna is now sitting alone with her Jack-and-ginger. She goes back to the two remaining rumpled-shirt men at the other end of the bar and brings them both over to Lizzie and their friend. "If I had wanted to hook up with one of them, I suppose I would have. But I just wasn't interested. If I had been, I wouldn't have dragged them over to Lizzie," she laughs. "It's all about self-preservation."

She leaves Lizzie and Henry with their men and heads home to Dan Rather.

Jen

"I'M IN MY Roseanne phase," Jen reports in halfway through February. "I can't seem to change out of my sweats and my muk-luks."

Jen has an interview next week for a full-time job at a big studio, and she is already rebelling against what's ahead: a suit, pinched toes, washed hair, the alarm clock.

El Niño is still battering L.A. with a vengeance. Torrential rains are pelting the roof of her little house. The cats are hiding under the bed again. She turns on the TV and settles in for the "Monica watch." Monica Lewinsky has just returned home to her father's house in Brentwood, and a news channel is covering it live. Now

Monica is getting off her plane. Now Monica is hugging her dad in the airport. Now Monica is trying to pull into her driveway.

Jen calls Becca and says she is envious of Monica's exciting life.

"I think you need to start taking Saint John's wort," Becca tells her.

"I think I need my own Web site. Did I tell you who Stewart is seeing?"

"I think the novelty of your free life is wearing off," Becca says.

"I know. I sleep more than my cats. But I'm supposed to meet Dean for drinks later, so I'm going to get dressed today."

Becca doesn't like this. "Why don't you come to Karin's birthday party with me instead?"

Karin is a friend of Becca's from college. She recently wrote a script and Becca loved it, so she brought it to a production head at a small studio. The guy fell in love with it and asked Becca what it would take to get her to quit her job and produce it independently. She told him she would have to think about it.

Alex and Becca have been talking about having kids, and Becca knows from her friends that stress is a big problem when it comes to getting pregnant. Getting a production deal is like starting your own business—you never clock out. But getting her own production deal would be a dream come true. Having children would be another dream come true. How can she choose between them?

KARIN'S PARTY IS at a Morroccan restaurant in Silver Lake. Jen arrives late, by herself, and wanders through a maze of dark hallways searching for familiar faces. A hostess finally escorts her to a private room in the back. There are silhouettes of women sitting on pillows around a table. "Karin?" she says into the dark.

"Jen!" she hears what sounds like Kate whispering loudly from the other side of the room. "Come over here and sit down."

Jen is making her way through the dark over to the outlined people when a light comes on over her head and *The Full Monty* soundtrack starts blasting from a speaker behind her. "*I believe in miracles . . .*" Hot Chocolate starts singing. Suddenly she feels a big body pressed up against her back, and soon her feet are in the air, spinning around the room. She looks up to see a bare-chested man grinning down at her. He looks a little like Joey Buttafuoco, and Jen starts screaming. Next thing you know she is on the floor, and Joey Buttafuoco is on top of her, doing what she hopes are push-ups. They are actually pelvic thrusts. She can't really see because she has covered her face with her hands. *"You sexy thing . . ."* the speakers are blasting. *"Where did you come from . . . ?"* The man tries to pry her arms open and Jen screams louder, until she starts to laugh. She can hear Kate and the women howling across the room as a flashbulb goes off. She curls herself up into a ball, then crawls out from under the man and runs over to the table with the others. The man follows her over to the table, gyrating and massaging himself for their . . . enjoyment. It turns out that each of the women received his special treatment when she entered the room. Karin decided after her bachelorette party two years ago that strippers are wasted on the engaged. She wanted to cheer up her friends.

When the dancing comes to halt, Jen looks around and sees her sister — still doubled over laughing on her pillow. Her big sister let her get dry-humped by Joey Buttafuoco! In a public restaurant! This is Becca's cure for what ails her? Wait until she tells mom.

March

But is Ally McBeal really progress? Maybe if she lost her job and wound up a single mom, we could begin a movement again.

—Ginia Bellafonte,
Time magazine

[A woman] may wish to be viewed as an individual, not as a representative of her gender. Sadly, our society is one that cannot differentiate between someone's proving a point as a woman and proving herself as a person.

—Lauren Rutledge,
age sixteen, *Time* Letters Page

ANNA IS BACK in San Francisco, planning another trip: Aspen. It's time for her annual ski trip, only this year Gwen and her husband have decided to separate and Ness has opted out. Ness thinks Anna and Gwen would have a better time if they went without her.

Gwen and her husband met and married two years out of college. They had matching families and matching friends from school and everyone cheered when they ran through the falling rice together. Anna seems to be the only one who really understands why they are separating. There are no other people, no major sins, she explains. They're just not sure if they're right for each other anymore. "Life has a way of changing you," Anna explains. "She didn't know what she wanted to be when she met him. And she wasn't a vice president of development then." Gwen fell in love with her job, Anna explains, as it got better and her relationship got worse.

Relationships have a way of changing you, too, Anna continues. Gwen hadn't stayed in one place for nine years when she first met him. When they were in college, there was change every five months—new courses, new people, new professors. Gwen didn't realize how much she thrived on that. But after she turned thirty, she felt she needed more life phases, new semesters, the excitement of new challenges. She wanted to live in different cities, work for a different company, explore. Her husband wanted to stay close to home. "He's a great guy," Anna says. "And there's a lot to be said for someone who makes the best of things the way they are. But they are just different."

Gwen has been calling Anna a lot lately. She has become an insomniac, which is good for the time difference between the east coast and west coast. "No matter how much people know divorce is the right thing, it's still torture," Anna says. "You just want it to work once you're married. You've invested so much, and you don't want to think it was all a waste."

Gwen is thirty-five now, and she has always thought she wanted kids, and everyone is wondering why she picked now to get restless. What are the odds that she will meet someone and be married again by forty, they want to know.

"She just knows that it's not worth being miserable for," Anna explains for Gwen (and, really, for herself). "Kids are great if you have a great relationship to have them in."

But if you love your job, like your life, and don't have a coparent you can picture staying with for twenty more years, it's hard to imagine bringing kids into the picture.

"I JUST LOVE this place," Anna says to Gwen as they head to the gondola in Aspen. "It's like a Disney World for adults!" It's up to her to be especially chipper this year. She wants to show Gwen that life is an adventure on the other side.

They've just spotted one of Aspen's life-size cartoon characters, Ivana Trump. Now they are getting in line for the big ride up the mountain, and they have just spent ten dollars for a soda. Anna is giddy about the snow. "Can you believe it? Who knew it was winter?"

Once aboard the six-person gondola, they meet two women from a Canadian ski club. One of them is divorced, and Gwen stares over at her, carefully trying to gauge each facial expression. Her biggest fear is that she'll look back a year from now with terrible regret about what she had done, and she is trying to find confirmation in the woman's face that she's made the right decision. The women both work in pharmaceuticals in Toronto, and they invite Anna and Gwen to join their group later that night for dinner.

When they arrive at the Flying Dog Brew Pub, they spot their two new friends at a table of ten men and women, drinking big porters and eating Rocky Mountain trout. It is an unlikely assembly: young and old, peppy and sullen, dressed up and dressed down. In fact, they have little in common other than this annual ski trip, which they have taken together for the cut rate. But they seem to warm to each other as the evening goes on, cracking Canadian jokes, recounting each other's wipeouts.

After dinner, it's off to Club Soda. The group takes over the dance floor, forming a circle and taking turns crossing it. Gwen tries to do some sort of Scottish sword dance. Anna does the limbo. Then a man with Alan Alda hair approaches her and offers to buy her a drink, and they leave the dance floor together, headed for the bar. He is a physical therapist, leaving the next day. After a half-hour of exchanging personal histories, he starts making out with her at the bar. When he asks her if she wants to go "someplace quiet," she tells him she can't leave her friend. But they spend another half-hour making out like teenagers in a dark hallway near the bathrooms. "I think that should be a prerequisite," she tells Gwen on the walk home. "They have to be leaving the next day."

The second night, after spending the day skiing, they are both sore and hungover. Gwen has been putting on a good show, but she is still having trouble sleeping. She turns in early, leaving Anna at their expensive hotel bar surrounded by a sea of graying hair. "I look around the room and think, Do I look like a gold digger? I must. When did this place get so *old*? I guess ski bums don't hang out at the hotel bars." This is the price Gwen and Anna pay for having money.

The third day they meet two doctors from Chicago at a cash machine and spend the rest of the day skiing with them. The men drag Anna and Gwen to the expert slopes and by the time they reach the bottom, all four of them are covered in snow. On the final ride up on the lifts, the cardiologist asks Anna why she came to Aspen.

"It's sort of our annual college reunion. There are usually more of us."

"Mr. Anna didn't want to come?"

"*Ex*-Mr. Anna," she says, smiling.

"I like being able to explain that I'm divorced," she says later. "It answers the question everyone is thinking—what's wrong with you that you're thirty-three and skiing with your girlfriend in Aspen? People get it when you're divorced."

Anna and Gwen spend the night dancing with their respective doctors. With Gwen paired off, Anna and the cardiologist sneak out and head back to Anna's hotel room. They are half-undressed an hour later when Gwen knocks on the door. She couldn't bring herself to go home with her doctor. She's not quite ready for that.

After the doctors leave the next day, Anna and Gwen spend a day skiing by themselves. Anna gives Gwen more "adventure" talks and tells her to give herself some time to mourn. "It's going to be really hard at first," she says. "You have to accept that. There will be this big void and you will get really lonely and try to fill it with all the wrong people. But once you move past that, you'll start to feel this incredible weight lifted. And you'll get to know yourself for the first time in your adult life. You don't have to lie to anyone anymore — not even to yourself."

Jen

"YOU'RE HIRED." The words Jen has been fearing and anticipating for six months now are coming from her sister. "I want you to run everything," Becca tells her.

The production deal came through from the small studio, and Becca wants Jen in charge of the day-to-day show. She will be responsible for putting together three low-budget movies over the next two years. Becca hopes to be giving birth to a high-budget, real-life bouncing baby in that time frame. She doesn't think she can handle the stress of both, and the only person she truly trusts to manage the film deal is her sister.

Jen is ecstatic. She'd been depressed since the last studio interview; the studio wanted her to work on more teen thrillers. But she didn't go into the movie business just to be in the movie business. She went into it because she wanted to work on movies she could fall in love with.

"Did we get the green light on the movie about the prep school boys?" she asks, referring to one of the scripts Becca found.

"Start scouting sites outside Boston."

"You *rock*! My sister rocks. I cannot believe you pulled this off."

When she hangs up, Jen goes straight to her closet and starts pulling out the plastic-wrapped suits. She will donate them somewhere, but she will never wear them again. She is an independent now, an independent producer.

Jen skips her afternoon nap and starts making lists. For six months, she has had to create lists of nothing—the list of people to call to distract herself, the list of things she really doesn't have to do. Now she realizes she could have actually accomplished something—cleaned out her closets, painted her bedroom, fixed the dent in her car.

She grabs her credit card and drives to Venice. She has been waiting for this—permission to lose herself in a colorful boutique on Main Street. She buys two tight, knee-length skirts, three French-cut juicy shirts, and open-toe platforms. She is no longer a closed-toe working stiff.

On her way home, she meets Dean for lunch at the Farmers' Market. He seems genuinely excited about her job and offers to help look at their deal contract—free of charge. Then he offers to find her office space in his building.

After lunch she stops at the flower mart and buys two tomato seedlings for Becca's garden. Her life is about to get big again.

El Niño has finally let up on her roof, and the cats are sleeping in the sunny spot on the couch. She curls up with them, Rudy and Mamie collapsing onto her stomach, heavy as bell weights. They are not letting her go anywhere.

Casey

"I'M AFRAID I ruined the perfect ending to my year," Casey says. It's been three weeks since she said she could quit her job and have kids with Andrew. Now she sounds upset. "I thought I was going to wrap it all up in a bow."

After some prying, Casey comes clean. "I was really bad Wednesday night," she says. Now she sounds mischievous. She broke her code of ethics, she explains. She spent a night with a band member—one of the boys she gets paid to look after.

"I have no idea where it came from. I'm running around trying to line up this announcement, completely lost in the details of work. I'm a mess, but too busy to care. My boss left for his sabbatical, and I've had to take over and it's been a little hairy. But I came to work this week and looked around and said, 'These people are goofballs. I can do this.'"

Then one of the goofballs told her he needs her to go to a video shoot for one of his bands. She's pissed. She's supposed to be a boss now, sending other people out to baby-sit.

After the shoot, she takes the band and the crew out for dinner at their hotel. She sits down at the end of the table next to the cute bassist. He's about twenty-five and looks like a clean-cut Tommy Lee—Tommy Lee if he had gone to Princeton and played lacrosse. He was sweaty from playing, and his bangs were sticking to his forehead.

"First he started playing with my puffy coat," she says. "He kept hugging it. I left to go talk to some people, and he followed me like a puppy dog. He takes my hand while I'm talking to his manager and drags me to the bar and starts buying me drinks."

Pretty soon, everyone around them started to leave, and Casey and the musician waved good-bye from the bar. "We just stared at each other.

"I think I vampired his energy. Either that or I'm hitting my sexual peak. If I ever settle down with Andrew, I'll have to have lovers on the side. He's never around."

Casey and the bassist finish one more drink at the bar, then take the hotel elevator to the top floor on a mission to find the roof. They end up kissing in an ice machine room instead. He interrupts in order to ask her what her favorite food is. Blueberries, she tells him. Soon they are in his hotel room, and he's dialing room service, ordering blueberries. "Dude, you've got to find me blueberries," she hears him say. "Look, you're lettin' me down, *man*." An hour later, a man knocks on their door carrying a silver tray with nothing but blueberries. Casey hides. She doesn't want to be caught in a hotel room with one of her musicians. She might end up on Page Six. The bassist gives the man a twenty-dollar tip, and Casey yells "Thank you!" from the bathroom.

"He's very proud of himself for pulling this off," she says, chuckling. "Very much 'in control,' which is good, because up until then, I'd been the powerful older woman. Bass players are not the most brilliant of the bunch. Little accomplishments are good."

The rest of the night is full of only little accomplishments. "When you know you only have one night, you throw yourself into it. But he was like a drunk college boy—no control, and it was like 'oops.' Then an hour later, he's all excited again, but he tells me he doesn't have any condoms. 'What are you thinking?' I say. 'You're a *musician*.' I tell him there was no way we were having sex. 'Okay,' he says. Then he says he's kind of glad. He wants us to have something to look forward to."

They're awakened early the next morning by the band's manager. "I'm kind of with someone," the bassist says into the phone. "I know, I know. Can I call you later?" He tells Casey when he hangs up that his manager said to stay away from the record company women. Something might go wrong, he said, and then the band could be screwed.

She gets to work at eleven the next day, her teeth blue from the berries. She wants to call Maggie and tell her about it, but she knows it would be too hard for Maggie to keep to herself; Maggie knows the band's manager. Beth gets the call instead.

"I think I just needed to get it out of my system," Casey tells Beth after her confession.

"I don't know, Case. Sounds as if he might have whetted your appetite." Beth is impressed.

"I know. I've had a taste of Turkish delight."

"It's hard to go back."

"Beth," Casey says, closing her office door. "This could really ruin my reputation around here. I've never hooked up with one of our artists. What if his manager tells someone?"

"He is not going to tell anyone. And so what if he does? It never hurt Stefan's reputation. Or Tommy Mottola's."

"Yeah, no shit. That's what *made* their reputations."

"How does that work? We hook up with the talent and we're like a masseuse. Tommy Mottola hooks up with Mariah Carey and he becomes Michael Corleone."

Casey decides she wouldn't want to be the Godfather. "How would you like it if the only reason people hooked up with you was because they were afraid not to?"

BY THE END of the day, Casey decides that the bassist is actually her "masseuse." "He definitely put something back into me that I'm going to need, to get into the work demands. I've got to get revved up about something if I am going to take on all of my boss's work for four more months."

What happened to getting revved up about Andrew? "I'm definitely losing steam on that one. He calls only once a week, when he's ready to see me. And the truth is, he's just so . . . uptown. The thing about musicians that I've always forgotten—they're very free and open and spontaneous. I'm attracted to that. That's why I wanted to work in the business in the first place."

Then Casey remembers her policy, her warnings about the artist ego, about fawning fans, about talking yourself out of jealousy. "It's true," she allows. "You can never expect a monogamous relationship. But could I even expect that from myself? Maybe that's not what we want."

When she checks in two days later, Casey admits that she can't really imagine dating the musician. "I know that it was just a fling. But Friday afternoon I had this daydream: I start dating the bassist. Things heat up between us. I kick out my roommate. He moves in. Then he goes on tour. And I've got the apartment to myself!"

Anna

"ARE WE DONE yet? I'm tired." Anna is ready to call it a year. She is exhausted from being a single subject. It's starting to feel like a job to her. Besides, she explains, it's hard to live in the moment when you have to record it. Too much pressure.

"I had all those years of being calm and pacified by Greg, and by the end I really felt I was missing something, missing out. So now I've had three years of living large, pushing the envelope all the time, trying everything out. I've had plenty of high drama. But I really do think I want to settle into my life."

Last week she visited the therapist again. She told the woman that she wanted to focus on big Anna. Then she announced that big Anna does not want to be alone her whole life. It's just that she's having a little trouble forcing this relationship thing. She listed all the *un*settling men she has seen since she separated from Greg: Ethan, Derek, Spencer, the CD-ROM man. She has not exactly made progress with relationships.

"If I really wanted to meet a husband guy, I'd go hang out in the Peninsula, right?" she asked the woman. "Silicon Valley is where all the bachelors are. They're all smart and rich and lonely for women."

"So why don't you?" the therapist said.

"Because it's not me."

"But how do you know that?"

"I don't," Anna conceded. "I know, I have to switch my thinking. I don't want to be with assholes my whole life. But I can't force it.

Not even for kids. I would probably kill myself if I was with some-one who just . . . wasn't me. I need humor."

"I'm sure there are plenty of funny men in the Peninsula."

Anna wrinkled her forehead and nodded. That's when she de-cided she was done with therapy. And relationships.

When she got to work the next day, she announced to Lizzie that she was off men. "You can't say that in this city," Lizzie told her.

"I'm not *on* women. But I'm committed to the off-men thing. I don't have time. And I'm determined that meeting someone will not dictate my life. No more trying to stick these round pegs through square holes."

Lizzie borrowed a magic marker and wrote "Off Men" on a sticky and stuck it to the front of Anna's desk.

The next day, Ted popped his head in and told her that the smart-ass actor from Chicago was moving to town.

"Ted," she said biting her lip and pointing to the front of her desk. "I don't think you saw my sign."

A sexy smart-ass guy who lives in San Francisco and might ac-tually *get* her? No way. Then she would have the perfect ending.

Jen

PAMELA AND TOMMY LEE just announced they are splitting up. Things were not so great off-camera, it turned out. So much for Hollywood charm.

Becca and Jen are in Becca's bedroom getting ready for a big party at Kate's. They want to celebrate their good news. Becca hands a glass of wine to Jen. "I have the perfect top for you," she says, pulling a small piece of folded cloth out of her dresser drawer. She drapes it on Jen's bare chest and ties it around her neck.

"It looks like a hanky with a choker!" Jen whines when she sees the backless halter top.

"The ski-hat man is not going to be able to take his eyes off you."

"I look ridiculous, and I'm bloated. Can't I just wear a juicy T?"

"No. Everyone else walks around like this. You have to flaunt it." That said, Becca pulls on a tight brown sateen dress that dips to show cleavage. Then she steps into a pair of shiny brown platforms.

About a hundred people are milling around Kate's backyard when they get there, with fifty more spilling out of her house onto her porch. The place is lit up with yellow and orange and blue patio lights. A DJ is playing "Rapper's Delight," and Kate's boyfriend's band is setting up on the lawn.

Becca and Jen make their way through the crowded living room to a peak spot on the porch. They have a view of the yard crowd and the porch people and the living room. They are talking about setting up office space and hiring an assistant, and Jen is not even looking around the party.

But Becca is. "There's a man who keeps walking by and staring up at you," she says, interrupting them. "He keeps checking out your back."

"Is he wearing a ski hat?"

"No. He's kind of preppy. He looks like Danny from *Zoom*. Don't look. He's staring right now."

"You really are a full-service agent. One-stop shopping. Do you have my lines ready for the ski hat?"

"Ask him about his pit bulls. Kate said he has two and he's really into them."

"*Hey*, there," the preppy guy has approached. He leans over and kisses Jen on the cheek.

"Oh, hi," she says, flustered. It's Griffin, the Luke Skywalker lookalike from her old job. Danny from *Zoom*? "I have *got* to get new lenses."

"Where have you *been*?" he says.

"Oh, all over the place, actually. This is my sister Becca." Becca holds out her hand and beams.

"He's from Boston," Jen tells her.

"So are we," Becca says, grinning wider.

"You look great," he says, looking Jen up and down. "I never see you out."

Jen smiles at him, then spots what she thinks is a ski hat over his shoulder.

"Are you coming down to see the band?" he asks.

"Uh, yeah, definitely. We're coming down in a few minutes."

"Who was that?" Becca asks after he leaves.

"That was Luke-alike. Apparently he can only talk to me when it's dark. He didn't say two words to me when we worked together."

"I think I should up my commission."

"Quick—I need some lines."

"I told you, pit bulls."

"Hi, Marsha," a deep voice says behind them. "Who's taking Marsha Brady to the prom?" It's Dean, and he's alone.

"Hey, it's my brother Greg," Jen says, trying to stick her fingers in her pocketless pants. Becca excuses herself, and Jen and Dean head to the drinks table together. She is so happy to see him. She was starting to fill up with dread about talking to the ski-hat man.

They walk around the party together, talking about her new "indie" life. He offers again to look at their production-deal contract. Then he trails off.

"What's wrong?" she asks.

"Huh? Oh . . . nothing."

They head outside to see the band, and Jen spots the man with the ski hat standing in the corner. She leans back and hides behind Dean. A half-hour later, when the band takes its first break, Dean corners her by the bathroom and tells her he is afraid that his marriage is falling apart. She puts her knuckles to her mouth and stares at him.

"That is so sad," is all she can think to say.

"I can't talk about this," he tells her.

They stand next to each other for two more songs, quietly watching the band. Then he leaves. Jen heads to the nearest bathroom, closes herself inside, and cups her hands over her ears. Then she searches the party for Becca.

"I need to talk to you," she says, interrupting her conversation.

"What?" Becca is angry. "I was talking to someone," she scolds as Jen pulls her away.

"He told me his marriage is falling apart."

"Dean?"

"He told me he couldn't talk about it. Then he changed the subject."

"Listen," Becca says, gripping Jen's arm. "If he's dumping his wife, then you don't want him." She pauses to sigh, then starts biting her cuticles. "I don't think I want to tell Alex this."

"DEAN IS BREAKING up with his wife," Becca tells Alex anyway, the following night when Jen comes over for dinner. "He's gone Hollywood on her. Jen, I always knew that guy was an asshole."

"Just because he's getting a divorce does not make him an asshole," Alex says, shaking his head. "We don't know what's going on between them, what kind of problems they have. For all we know *she* wants out."

"Look, I'm sure it's just a rough spot," Jen says. "They'll work through it."

WHAT HAPPENS WHEN the perfect unavailable man threatens to become available? What happens when your fantasy life is co-opted by reality life? Where do you go to hide then?

Jen likes her life, simple and light. She has her cat-kids and her sitter-sister and her Potsy date. She has spas and bikes and trips and hikes. She has her sanity. She has "home" to re-create on a very big screen.

She's used to being alone, maybe because she has to be, maybe because she just likes it. She came into the world alone, after all, and for most of her thirty years she's had a bed all to herself. She was a really happy kid, and she didn't have a soulmate then. She didn't even know what a soulmate was. (Come to think of it, she's still not sure.)

And now she is grounded by her cats, attached to her work, close to her family, physical with a masseuse.

Maybe someday she will be ready to give all this up for something, someone. Maybe it will even be Dean. Or maybe she will just remain on the loose. Either way, she knows she will be okay, happy ever after.

Casey

NOT EVEN A week after her night with the bassist, Casey gets a call from one of her bosses. "Your band boys are so bad," he says. "I just read in the gossip columns that the bassist had a wild night Saturday with a model."

"I know, they're so bad," Casey agrees. "I've got to go now." She runs out and picks up the New York tabloids.

After a couple of hours, she calls to tell the story. "I was just feeling like such an asshole." Her blueberry boy hooked up with a magazine-cover girl. "It's so bad it's good," she says, breathing heavily into the phone. "I mean — slam dunk. I didn't even get a week!" And it wasn't as if she hadn't warned herself about musicians. "I know, I set myself up for this one. But Christ, to read about him hooking up with a model in the paper three days later? I was lucky I didn't go on a two-hour shopping spree to make myself feel better."

At dinner the following week for her year-end wrap-up, Casey shows up with a stuffy nose from allergies. It's hot out, Indian spring, and the air is thick with humidity and pollen. She talks about the latest item in the New York Post: her bassist is still "canoodling" with his new woman all over town. She is laughing. "I'm thinking, well at least he's made my job easier. Any publicity for the band is great. And he has good taste. I like her. I'm so big."

Her whirlwind year is over, and she is steadying herself. She is gathering it all up, gathering up a perspective. How did she go from talking about kids with Andrew to discovering that her one-night stand is cheating on her by reading about it in the paper?

"I don't know. I think all this focusing on relationships and worrying about the big one has just made me a little nuts. It's not fun, and it's not doing me any good. There is no huge need for that right now."

It turns out that Casey was under the impression that this "single girl" project was all about her search for the big one—a husband. But she admits that she didn't seem very worried about it most of the year. "There are so many people around me who it hasn't happened for—meeting someone special. I honestly wonder if it's going to happen to me. I went into things with Bruce thinking it would go on forever. But I could never really imagine it. I don't consider myself a commitment-phobe; I've been at ease in relationships. But a wall does go up. At this point, it's mostly a way to cover myself. I know that. I know too many great people in this city who just haven't found anyone they want to marry. So I guess I'm preparing myself."

Part of preparing herself has been stepping outside herself, taking a look. "There's just no getting around it—I'm a late bloomer. I'm still really coming into my own. I've spent a good part of my adult life in serious relationships, always being the team player, always putting the relationship or somebody else first. But when you're by yourself, your experiences are different, and they have more of an impact on you. Being alone has made me get out there and meet people, and every person I've met has opened a new door for me . . .

"So maybe I didn't really have the chance to run around with cute bassists when I was twenty-four. Maybe now I'm just more confident, and I can handle these relationships. I can temper them with other distractions. I'm playing catch-up."

She still sees Andrew once a week, but she has lost her willingness to color him in. "There is some reason why Andrew and I keep going back to each other, but I don't know if it's a big reason. I think I was more interested in his interest in me than I was in him. He's a very cerebral, issue-laden man, and I will always take a backseat."

She also admits that it has never been essential to her to have kids, and this has taken a lot of the pressure off.

"And I'm very good at programming myself," she allows. "If Andrew had made more of an effort, I might not be cutting myself loose. But whatever, it's working. The fact that I don't know what's going to happen with that relationship used to seem scary to me. Now it seems okay. The fling with the bassist gave me a boost. You could just be going along through your day and never even know what's around the corner."

When she looks back at her year, she seems satisfied that she has lived it well, always finding something new around the corner. "I've been spoiled. I've definitely put in the effort and run around a lot, to the detriment of my health and career and home—my apartment's a mess. But the dating thing has been pretty damn good for me when I've wanted it to be."

The problem is, maybe, that it's been too good for her. She admits that, after almost two years of being string-free, she's still addicted to the fall. "I was hoping I'd get over it. It's so easy to fall into a shallow, heady, lusty love each time. But the bassist made me realize—I'm not over it.

"But I'm happy with this light phase right now. Does it ever last? I do still believe in looking for a soulmate. But when do I stop? And how do I know?" For a couple of minutes she is content to leave her questions unanswered. But then her forehead starts to crease. "Who knows, maybe Stefan and I will end up together when he's seventy and I'm sixty."

For now, Casey seems to be lost in her new job responsibilities. With her boss on leave, she has a chance to come up with her own ideas and make them happen. She's spent a long time waiting for this. She's finally a leader.

"The bottom line is, I have this incredible job and this great opportunity to really do something with it right now. I'm in charge, and I like it."

Beth has been dragging her to a new yoga class. The focus is less on exercises and more on meditation. It borrows a lot from Buddhism, Casey explains. "The yogi sits at the front of the room and talks to the class in a soothing voice. He tells us that we have to bow to our inner selves, that everything we need is right here within us.

"You have to take responsibility for your own happiness," she says outside the restaurant after the wrap-up. The trees in her Greenwich Village neighborhood are covered in white blossoms. "When I was twenty-six, I used to yearn for things I didn't have. Now I look at what I do have. I have a great life."

She stops to sneeze. "Things are good. I'm happy. I hope this doesn't screw up your story."

Epilogue

IT REALLY WASN'T a good year for intimacy. People who became intimate quickly became out-imate: Kelly Flinn, Frank Gifford, Sergeant-Major McKinney, Pamela and Tommy, Monica Lewinsky . . .

It really wasn't a good year for marriage. People who were married got taxed, investigated, slandered, fired, humiliated, exiled, subpoenaed, and indicted.

It was a great year to be a single woman in the world, however. Single women were celebrated on the covers of magazines (Madonna, Sandra Bullock, Minnie Driver, Gwyneth Paltrow, Sheryl Crow), and in sitcoms (*Suddenly Susan, Friends, Ally McBeal*). And outside of the military, single women were allowed to fraternize with whomever they pleased. Audiences even preferred that single women stay single: during test screenings of the hit *My Best Friend's Wedding,* audiences in the Midwest said they did not want Julia Roberts to end up marrying Dermott Mulroney at the end. They wanted her to end up with the fun gay dancer.

It wasn't all fun and dancing for Anna, Jen, and Casey. There were plenty of lumps—letdowns and loneliness. And all that freedom and possibility can be exhausting.

But as easy as it is to poke fun at their seventies childhoods, the politics of the time provided them with coed opportunities and coed expectations, and now they are free to recognize and acknowledge a very coed yearning for something beyond a ring, a secure nest, and a good wage-earner. It has given them the freedom to be alone. And it has given them the freedom to fall in love—on their own terms and set by their own clocks.

Acknowledgments

THANKS FIRST AND FOREMOST to Anna, Casey, and Jen for their stories and their time, their humor and their wisdom.

Thanks to my editor, Ann Treistman, for conceiving this idea, shaping it, and taking a gamble on me. I'm grateful, too, for the support of Henry Ferris at William Morrow.

And to Karen Avrich, Patty Jones, John Kelly, Heather Long, Lauren MacIntyre, and Elizabeth Sheinkman for their insights and feedback. Also thanks to Jen Bradley, Michael Carroll, Rich Cohen, Tennley DaVia, Sara Eckel, Tad Floridis, Stephanie Kiefer, Alison Klapper, Ned Martel, Tobias Perse, Rose Tobin, and Bryant Urstadt. And special thanks to Tom Conroy and Mike Rubiner, for the first break.

Finally, thanks to my dad, Rich Roth, for all the input and encouragement, and to my mom, Mary Beth Ross, for years of edits, articles, books, and assurances.